INQUIRY
SCIENCE

Grades 4–5

Published by
Frank Schaffer Publications®

Editor: Karen Thompson

Frank Schaffer Publications®

Printed in the United States of America. All rights reserved. Limited Reproduction Permission: Permission to duplicate these materials is limited to the person for whom they are purchased. Reproduction for an entire school or school district is unlawful and strictly prohibited. Frank Schaffer Publications is an imprint of School Specialty Publishing. Copyright © 2006 School Specialty Publishing.

Send all inquiries to:
Frank Schaffer Publications
3195 Wilson Drive NW
Grand Rapids, Michigan 49534

Inquiry Science—grades 4-5

ISBN 0-7682-3374-7

2 3 4 5 6 7 8 9 MAZ 10 09 08 07 06

Table of Contents

Table of Contents

0-7682-3374-7 *Inquiry Science*

Electricity&Magnetism

0-7682-3374-7 *Inquiry Science*

Magnetic Attraction

Gearing Up

Open a can in front of the class with an electric can opener. Lead the students to wonder why the can stayed suspended while the can opener worked. A magnet holds the can in place. You may wish to carefully allow each child a chance to attach a can to the can opener. Brainstorm other familiar things that might contain a magnet.

Process Skills Used
- predicting
- recording data
- observing
- classifying
- graphing

Guided Discovery

Background for the teacher:

A magnet is an object that attracts (brings near) metals such as iron and steel. The ends of a magnet are called poles. A magnet has a north pole and a south pole. Opposite poles attract; the north pole of one magnet attracts the south pole of another magnet. Like poles repel; the north pole of one magnet pushes away the north pole of another magnet.

Materials needed for each group:

magnets

objects to explore: wood block, thread, steel pin, aluminum foil, copper wire, paper clip, penny, shoelace, plastic straw, steel wool, nail, metal can, metal spoon

Directions for the activity:

Have students fill in the prediction column of the data table to indicate whether items will be attracted to magnets. Then, allow them time to explore and find out which items are attracted to magnets. Have the students sort the objects into two groups: items that are attracted to magnets, and those that are not.

Responding to Discovery

Lead students to make conclusions as to what items are attracted to magnets. Help students to realize that all metals are not magnetic.

Applications and Extensions

Think about how magnets are used to make our lives easier. Write about some magnets we use in everyday life.

Real-World Applications
- Discuss how inventors use magnets.
- Discuss when you wouldn't want a metal to be magnetic.

0-7682-3374-7 *Inquiry Science*

Magnetic Attraction

☙ First, make a prediction, then test each item. Hold each item next to the magnet to determine whether it is magnetic. Write your observations below on the chart.

Item	Your prediction	Is it magnetic?	What is it made of?
wood block			
thread			
steel pin			
aluminum foil			
copper wire			
paper clip			
penny			
shoelace			
steel wool			
nail			
metal can			
metal spoon			
plastic straw			

☙ Were there any items that surprised you? _____

☙ What did you observe about the magnetic items?_____

☙ Sort the items into two groups. Draw a picture of each item in its proper category.

magnetic	non-magnetic

0-7682-3374-7 *Inquiry Science*

Making a Compass

Gearing Up

You probably have the walls in your classroom labeled north, south, west, and east. Ask the students to explain how they know the north wall is north other than "My teacher says it is." Lead them to ask for proof. You can provide proof with a compass. Obtain several different styles of compasses to show that they all point to north.

> ### Process Skills Used
> • following directions
> • observing
> • recording data

Guided Discovery

Background for the teacher:

The compass has been used for a long time to help navigators find directions. A magnetic compass is an instrument that indicates direction. The compass needle always points to the magnetic North Pole. When you have established north, you can determine the other directions by their relationship to north. In this lesson, students will make their own compass.

Materials needed for each group:

a magnet   straight pin

small square of Styrofoam
(from a meat tray)

plastic bowl   water

loose staples in a dish
(one for the whole class)

Directions for the activity:

Demonstrate to students that the pin is not a magnet by holding the pin in a container of loose staples. Then have each group rub the head of a pin back and forth 40 times on one side of the magnet. Then have them put their magnetized pins in the dish of staples again to show that it is now a magnet. Once the pin is magnetized, students poke it through the Styrofoam square so that the pin is sticking out on both sides. Float the Styrofoam with the pin in a horizontal position in a bowl of water. The water should be just deep enough so that the pin and Styrofoam move freely. Be sure that all magnets are put away as they will interfere with the compass. Instruct the students to turn the pin in either direction. They will find that it will turn back to the original direction. The pin is pointing to north and south poles.

Responding to Discovery

Ask students what might happen if a magnet were placed near the pin once it was in the water.

Applications and Extensions

How might a compass be useful for finding constellations?

> ### Real-World Applications
> • Discuss how hikers use a compass and a map.
> • Discuss how pilots use a compass to navigate.

0-7682-3374-7 *Inquiry Science*

Making a Compass

❧ Draw what happened when your teacher held a pin in a pile of loose staples.

❧ Magnetize the pin by rubbing it back and forth 40 times on one side of a magnet. Draw what happened when you held the magnetized pin in a pile of loose staples.

❧ Poke the magnetized pin sideways through the styrofoam and place it in a small amount of water. Draw the pin in the water and label the directions (north, south, west, and east).

❧ Turn the floating pin a half turn and let it go. Explain what happened.

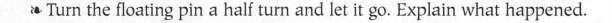

_____

❧ How is what you created like a compass? _____

_____

Mapping a Magnet

Gearing Up

Obtain several different maps. Include road maps, classroom and school maps, state and world maps. Discuss ways that maps can be helpful.

Guided Discovery

Background for the teacher:

Just as the earth has a north and a south pole, a magnet also has a north and south pole. If a magnet is broken in half, it will still have a north and a south pole. You can use a compass to map, or label, the poles of a magnet.

Materials needed for each group:

two magnets

one compass

12 cm of masking tape

pen or pencil

Directions for the activity:

Demonstrate how to map the poles of a magnet. Place 1 inch of masking tape on each end or side of the two mag-

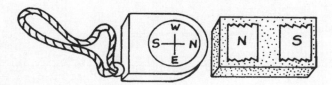

nets. Hold one end/side of the magnet to the side of the compass. Observe the compass needle. Write N or S on the masking tape to indicate the compass direction (north or south). Flip the magnet and hold the magnet to the compass again. Label the other side of the magnet. Have the students repeat these steps to map, or label, their two magnets. Allow groups time to explore how the north and south poles react to each other and different magnetic surfaces.

Responding to Discovery

Discuss how the north and south poles react to each other and different magnetic surfaces.

Applications and Extensions

Do magnets work under water? Through clothing? Test the attraction of opposite poles of the magnets through different substances.

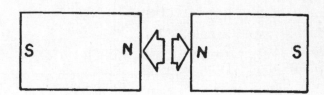

0-7682-3374-7 *Inquiry Science*

Name _____

Mapping a Magnet

1. Place 2-3 cm of masking tape on each end or side of the two magnets.

2. Hold one end/side of the magnet to the side of the compass.

3. Observe the compass needle. Write N or S on the masking tape to indicate the compass direction (north or south).

4. Flip the magnet and hold the magnet to the compass again. Label the other side of the magnet.

5. Repeat these steps to "map" or label the second magnet.

❧ Explore how the north and south poles react to each other and different magnetic surfaces.

1. Hold the "N" of one magnet to the "N" of the other magnet.

   Did the magnets attract or repel? _____

2. Hold the "S" of one magnet to the "S" of the other magnet.

   Did the magnets attract or repel? _____

3. Predict what will happen when the "S" of one magnet is placed next to the "N" of the other magnet. _____

4. Test your prediction and explain what happened. _____
   _____

5. Draw a picture of two magnets that are attracted to each other.

6. Draw a picture of two magnets that repel each other here.

0-7682-3374-7 *Inquiry Science*

Magnetizing Metals

Gearing Up

Hold up two forks and ask the class to tell you what they are. They should say "forks." Tell them that they are mistaken; it is a flashlight. Arrange the forks so they touch the bottom and top of a battery and light a bulb. Let's explore today how we can make another everyday object perform a new task.

Process Skills Used

- observing
- recording data
- predicting
- forming a hypothesis

Guided Discovery

Background for the teacher:

Some metals can be magnetized so that they function as a magnet. A steel straight pin is magnetized by rubbing it on a magnet in one direction. The more stokes against the magnet, the greater the magnetic strength.

Material needed for each group:

a steel pin for each student

a bar magnet (more than one per group is nice)

small paperclips

Safety tip: warn students to be careful with the sharp end of the pin.

Directions for the activity:

Before beginning, instruct students to hold their pins in a pile of paper clips to show that the pins are not magnetic. Each student strokes the side of a pin across the top of the magnet about 50 times in one direction (not back and forth). Then, students place the pin inside the pile of paper clips again and count how many clips are picked up.

Responding to Discovery

Ask students to describe what happened. Discuss how a magnet can pass it's magnetism to another object. Discuss why students think they must stroke in one direction only. Discuss why they must stroke so many times. Discuss what other objects they could magnetize.

Applications and Extensions

Have students explore other objects in the classroom to determine what objects can be magnetized.

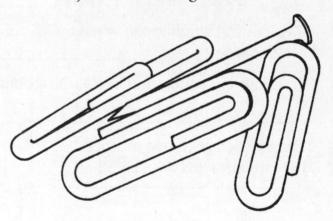

Real-World Applications

Discuss how high-speed trains in Japan and Germany use magnets to operate. The trains are magnetically propelled across the tracks at a very high speed of up to 500 km per hour.

 0-7682-3374-7 *Inquiry Science*

Name _____

Magnetizing Metals

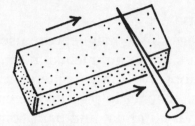

🍃 Stroke the pin across the magnet 50 times in one direction. Hold the magnetized pin in the paper clips. Count how many paperclips the pin picked up.

_____

🍃 What do you think will happen if you stroke the magnet more than 50 times?

_____

🍃 Stroke a pin 75 times across a magnet. How many clips did you get this time?

_____

🍃 Do you think you can magnetize other materials? Make a list of materials you would like to try. Predict what will happen and try to magnetize the items. Record your observations.

Item	Prediction	How many clips did it pick up?
_____	_____	_____
_____	_____	_____
_____	_____	_____
_____	_____	_____

🍃 Do you think it makes a difference if you stroke the pin toward the north or south pole of the magnet? _____

What steps do you need to go through to test your hypothesis? _____

_____

_____

Try your hypothesis.

0-7682-3374-7 *Inquiry Science*

Magnetic Fields

Gearing Up

Very strong magnets are used to lift cars and other metals in scrap metal shops. A strong magnetic field allows the magnet to pick up the car. Hold your hand flat and pour some iron filings in the palm of your hand. Pass a magnet under your hand. Did the magnetic field go through your hand to move the filings?

> ### Process Skills Used
> - recording data
> - observing
> - predicting
> - classifying
> - communicating

Guided Discovery

Background for the teacher:

The earth is surrounded by a magnetic field. Imagine there is a large bar magnet buried inside the earth. The poles of this imaginary magnet are located near the North and South poles. Scientists think that the Earth's magnetism may be produced from the huge iron core and the rapid spinning of the earth.

Material needed for each group:

iron filings

plastic baggie to hold the magnet

bar magnet

materials: glass jar, aluminum pan, thin block of wood, paper, water in a sealed plastic bag

Directions for the activity:

Students will test whether the bar magnet can move the iron filings through the different materials listed on the chart on page 15.

Teacher tip: Have students put their magnet in the baggie. If the iron filings touch the magnet, simply remove the magnet from the bag and the filings will fall off. Otherwise, it is very difficult to remove the filings from the magnet.

Responding to Discovery

Have students calculate the percentage of their correct predictions. Discuss what the results say about the ability of magnetic fields to pass through different materials. Discuss what students actually observed that told them the magnetic field passed through the material.

Applications and Extensions

Change the thickness of the materials in the experiment to determine whether that makes a difference in the magnetic field passing through it.

> ### Real-World Applications
> Magnets are now being used to clean fish tanks. One magnet is placed on the outside of the glass and one is placed on the inside. The magnet penetrates the glass and moves back and forth to clean the tank.

0-7682-3374-7 *Inquiry Science*

Name _____

Magnetic Fields

❧ Before you test each item, make your predictions on the chart. Place the filings on one side of the material. Place the magnet on the other side. Observe whether the magnetic field passes through the material.

Item	Your prediction	Item's response
paper	_____	_____
wood	_____	_____
glass	_____	_____
aluminum	_____	_____
plastic	_____	_____
water in a sealed bag	_____	_____

❧ Draw a picture for each item to show how the filings responded.

<table>
<tr><td></td><td></td><td></td></tr>
<tr><td></td><td></td><td></td></tr>
</table>

0-7682-3374-7 *Inquiry Science*

Are All Metals Magnetic?

Gearing Up

Have you ever wondered if all metals are equally magnetic? Try this simple test to see. Try to pick up a quarter with a magnet. Now try a steel pin. Was there a difference?

Process Skills Used
- predicting
- calculating
- recording data
- graphing
- experimenting
- following directions

Guided Discovery

Background for the teacher:

Most materials, even wood, copper, and water do not seem to respond to magnets. Actually, all materials can respond to magnetic force, but some so weakly that the force is not observable in everyday life. Items that respond well to magnets are iron, nickel, and cobalt.

Materials for each group:

magnet

sharpened pencil (graphite)

straight pin (steel)

aluminum foil

copper wire

paper clip (steel)

penny (copper-plated zinc)

steel wool

nail (iron)

aluminum can

dime (copper and nickel)

Directions for the activity:

Students test each of the items for its reaction to the magnet. Have students complete the table. They should research the composition of the different metal items (content is in parentheses in the materials list).

Responding to Discovery

Study and discuss the completed table. Have students determine what types of metals are always magnetic. What types of metals are not attracted to the magnet?

Applications and Extensions

Have students collect as many different metals as they can find. From what they know about different types of metals, have them predict which ones will be attracted to a magnet and which ones will not.

Real-World Applications
Discuss how mechanics may magnetize their screwdrivers to retrieve lost screws.

0-7682-3374-7 *Inquiry Science*

Are All Metals Magnetic?

☙ List the items being tested in the table. Predict and then test each item against a magnet. Record whether each item is magnetic or nonmagnetic.

Item	Your prediction	Is it magnetic?	What is it made of?

☙ Research the items to determine their composition. Study the table.

What types of metals are always magnetic?

_____

What types of metals are never magnetic?

_____

Is There Really Iron in Cereals?

Gearing Up

Discuss with students that their parents probably want them to eat cereal that contains vitamins and minerals because vitamins and minerals are healthy. Reproduce the nutritional information on two boxes of iron-fortified cereal, such as Total and Quaker oatmeal. Have students find out how much of each mineral is in the cereals and what percentage that is of the recommended daily allowance.

> ### *Process Skills Used*
> - reading a table
> - observing
> - recording data

Guided Discovery

Background for the teacher:

In this experiment, students are separating a mixture. Students have learned that iron is a magnetic material. This will help them come up with a plan for removing iron from the cereal. In separating minerals from rocks, other methods include acidic or caustic water, gravity separation, or flotation. For example, gravity separation is used in gold panning. Students will be surprised to find that their cereal contains iron filings.

Materials for each pair or group:

1 cup (237 ml) iron-fortified cold cereal (Total)

2 cups (474 ml) hot water

one clear drinking glass

a bar magnet wrapped in plastic wrap secured with a twistie

Directions for the activity:

Select a sample of cereal that is iron-fortified, such as Total. Students add hot water to make a slurry and stir with the magnet until the cereal is soggy. The longer the cereal is stirred, the more complete the iron removal. 30 minutes gives the maximum iron recovery. Students remove the magnet and remove the plastic wrap over a sheet of white paper. The particles of iron will fall to the paper. Hold the magnet below the paper to show that they are attracted to the magnet.

Responding to Discovery

Compare student findings. Compare how long students kept the magnets in the mixture to the amount of iron that was separated. Ask students how they think they could measure the amount of iron separated from the cereal.

Applications and Extensions

What other fortified food product could be used instead of cold cereal? What other methods could they use to separate the mixture?

> ### *Real-World Applications*
> - Discuss the importance of iron in the diet
> - Research how scientists find creative ways to separate mixtures

Name _____

Is There Really Iron in Cereals?

🔖 Look at the nutritional information on two different cereal boxes. Fill in the table to show how much of each mineral is present in each.

Mineral name	Cereal one	Cereal two
_____	_____	_____
_____	_____	_____
_____	_____	_____
_____	_____	_____
_____	_____	_____

🔖 Do you think you can measure the actual amount of iron in the cereal? To do this, you will need to separate the mixture that makes up the cereal. Follow the directions to separate the iron from the rest of the cereal.

1. Pour a cup of iron-fortified cereal in a glass.

2. Add hot water to make a slurry and stir with the magnet.

3. Keep track of how long you stir. Observe the dark slivers of iron attached to the magnetic bar. Remove the plastic wrap over a sheet of white paper.

How long did you stir the cereal? _____

Describe what you saw once the magnet was removed from the cereal. What do you think the black pieces are. How do you know? _____

_____

🔖 Repeat the experiment with the other cereal.

How long did you stir the cereal? _____

Describe what you saw once the magnet was removed from the cereal. _____

_____

 0-7682-3374-7 *Inquiry Science*

Exploring Electromagnets

Gearing Up

Touch a steel or iron nail to a pile of small paper clips. Did the nail pick up the paper clips? Discuss why it didn't. Ask the students if there might be a way to magnetize the nail. Try their suggestions. Then, tell them that today they will be making this nail into an electromagnet.

> ### *Process Skills Used*
> - observing
> - recording data
> - predicting
> - making a model
> - comparing

Guided Discovery

Background for the teacher:

Magnetism is produced by the motion of electrical charges. You can magnetize a conductor of electricity, such as a nail, by running current through the conductor. The more coils of wire that are wrapped around the nail, the stronger the electromagnet will become. The smaller the battery, the less magnetism will be produced.

Material needed per group:

one 6-volt lantern battery

large iron or steel nail

30 small paperclips

insulated wire cut in the following lengths: 35 cm, 50 cm, and 65 cm (Strip the insulation from both ends of the wires.)

Directions for the activity:

Show the students how to wrap a wire around the nail leaving 5 cm of wire unwrapped at each end. In each group, the students should tightly wrap the 35 cm wire around the nail.

Then, the students attach the wire ends to the different ends of the battery. (Be careful, some heat is given off.)

Students hold the pointed end of the nail in the pile of clips and lift. They record the number of paper clips picked up.

Students repeat the same process with each length of wire.

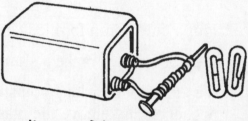

Responding to Discovery

Discuss what happened to the nail when the electric current ran around it.

Applications and Extensions

Discuss how students could change variables to increase or reduce the strength of the electromagnet (tighter or looser coils, larger or smaller nail, larger or smaller battery).

> ### *Real-World Applications*
> - Discuss how electromagnets are used in car starters, doorbells, can openers, and telephones.

0-7682-3374-7 *Inquiry Science*

Exploring Electromagnets

❧ Before the wire was attached to the battery, did the nail pick up any paper clips? Explain why or why not. _____

_____

Draw the nail wrapped in the wire attached to the battery.	Draw your electromagnet approaching a pile of paperclips.

❧ Record how many paper clips your electromagnet picked up.

Lenth of wire	Number of clips picked up
35 cm	_____
50 cm	_____
60 cm	_____

How many paper clips do you think a 80 cm wire electromagnet will pick up?

_____

❧ What else could you change to affect the number of paper clips your electromagnet picks up? _____

_____

❧ What could you use besides a nail to make an electromagnet? _____

_____

0-7682-3374-7 *Inquiry Science*

Recycled Battery Holder

Gearing Up:

Discuss the reasons why people recycle. The three Rs of recycling are reduce, reuse, and recycle. In today's activity, the students will reuse an empty toilet paper roll to make a recycled battery holder.

> *Process Skills Used*
> - following a sequence
> - measuring
> - communicating
> - making a model

Guided Discovery

Background for the teacher:

Rather than purchase a specialized battery holder for exploring electricity concepts, practice recycling by making this battery holder from an empty toilet paper roll.

Material needed for each holder:

D-cell battery

toilet paper tube

two 3 inch (7.5 cm) nails

two thick rubber bands

two sheets of aluminum foil

two 30 cm pieces of wire with stripped ends

two washers

strips of newspaper (width of battery)

Directions for the activity:

Students follow the directions on page 23 to make a recycled battery holder. In advance, you will need to strip the ends off the insulated wire with a knife. Guide students carefully through this experiment. Warn them to be careful with any sharp objects, such as the nails. There is potential for injury when they poke the nails through the tube. You may wish to have them work over a soft surface, such as Styrofoam to absorb the pressure.

Responding to Discovery

Ask students to trace how the energy from the battery moves through the conductors in this homemade battery holder. Have students propose explanations for why it is important to strip the ends of the insulated wire?

Applications and Extensions

Use the battery holder to light a bulb and demonstrate parallel and series circuits.

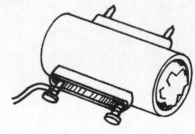

> *Real-World Applications*
> Compare how the body of a flashlight is like a battery holder.

0-7682-3374-7 *Inquiry Science*

Name _____

Recycled Battery Holder

1. Wrap newspaper strips around the battery so it will fit snugly in the tube. Be certain that the paper does not go past the ends of the battery.

2. Slide the wrapped battery into the center of the toilet paper tube. Mark the tube to indicate the positive and negative ends of the battery.

3. Gently crumple the aluminum foil. Place a foil ball in each end of the tube so they touch the ends of the battery.

4. Carefully push the nails through the walls of the tube and through the foil.

5. Put a rubber band over the two nails on each side. The rubber bands should be tight enough to put pressure on the nails.

6. Wrap one stripped end of each wire to the heads of the nails. Attach a washer to each of the loose ends.

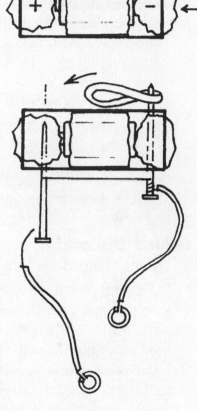

❧ Does the foil serve as a conductor or an insulator? _____

❧ What is the source of energy in this setup? _____

❧ Explain how the current passes from the battery to the washers.

_____

❧ Draw a picture of how you could use two battery holders together to light a bulb.

0-7682-3374-7 *Inquiry Science*

Flashing the Light

Gearing Up

Shine a flashlight around the room. Ask the students if they have ever taken apart a flashlight to see how it works. Talk about the setup of the flashlight as you take it apart. Note the arrangement of the batteries and the connection to the bulb. Point out how the switch connects and disconnects the circuit.

> ### Process Skills Used
> - making a model
> - predicting
> - forming a hypothesis
> - communicating

Guided Discovery

Background for the teacher:

A battery, otherwise known as a dry cell, is a source of energy. The larger the battery, the more energy that can be stored and used. By using multiple batteries, students can cause the light to burn brighter. Large electrical items, such as a radio, use more batteries than a flashlight. A D-cell battery is not strong enough to harm the students, although they might feel some heat given off. Inform students that they should not experiment with electrical outlets at home. They can get hurt using that type of electricity.

Material needed for each group:

one D-cell battery holder (see Recycled Battery Holder activity)

flashlight bulb

Directions for the activity:

Explain to students that the flow of electricity follows a circular path. When you turn on a light, you complete a circuit so an electric current can flow to a light bulb. Challenge the students to figure out how to light the bulb and form a complete circuit. Teacher tip: In order for the bulb to light, one washer must be on the contact point and the other washer should be on the metal casing that holds the bulb. **Note:** *if the attached washers repeatedly come in contact with each other, it could damage the battery.*

Responding to Discovery

Students draw pictures of the different arrangements they tried to light the bulb. Have them write a description of the arrangement that worked. Discuss the flow of energy in the circuit.

Applications and Extensions

Make a battery holder for three batteries using a paper towel roll.

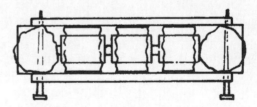

> ### Real-World Applications
> Demonstrate how different sized batteries are used for different size flashlights.

0-7682-3374-7 *Inquiry Science*

Name _____

Flashing the Light

❧ Draw a plan for how you will connect the bulb to your battery holder and light the bulb. Label all the parts.

❧ Explain how your drawing shows a complete circuit. Build your model.

_____

_____

❧ Try other arrangements until you make the bulb light. Draw the arrangement that works below. Label all the parts.

❧ Explain how your model completes the circuit._____

_____

❧ Bonus: Try another configuration using two battery holders.

Conductors and Insulators

Gearing Up

Ask the students to reflect on what they know about the flow of electricity in a circuit. Can they think of anything that would stop, or interrupt, the flow of electricity? Use a piece of tape to attach a wire to the bottom of a D-cell battery. Attach the other end to the side of a light bulb. Put your finger on top of the battery between the bulb and the battery. Ask the students to describe what happened and explain why.

> ### Process Skills Used
> - predicting
> - observing
> - drawing conclusions
> - recording data

Guided Discovery

Background for the teacher:

An item that stops electrons from flowing freely is called an insulator. An item that allows electric current to flow freely is called a conductor.

Materials needed per group:

one D-cell battery

20 cm of insulated wire with the ends stripped

one flashlight bulb

tape

potential conductors and insulators: eraser, Popsicle stick, sponge, pencil, paper, cardboard, plastic lid, penny, aluminum foil, metal key, metal washer, metal lid, steel wool, paper clip)

Directions for the activity:

Students will test the given items to determine whether they are conductors or insulators. They should look for similarities in the items that are insulators. Have them make predictions before testing the items. To set up the circuit, they can tape the stripped end of the wire to the bottom of the battery and tape the other end to the side of the metal base of the light bulb. Or use the recycled battery holder from a previous lesson.

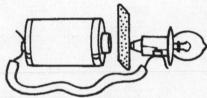

Responding to Discovery

Have students study their data. Discuss what the conductors have in common. Discuss what the insulators have in common. Can they make up a rule that would help identify which items are conductors and which are insulators? Discuss what this list has in common with the items that are magnetic.

Applications and Extensions

Think of ten additional items and predict whether they are conductors or insulators. Test each one.

> ### Real-World Applications
> Discuss how electrical wires are coated with plastic, which acts as an insulator.

0-7682-3374-7 *Inquiry Science*

Conductors and Insulators

Big Question: Which items are conductors and which are insulators?

1. Tape the stripped end of the wire to the bottom of the battery. Tape the other end to the side of the metal base of the light bulb.

2. Predict whether each item is a conductor or an insulator.

3. Test each item by placing the item between the battery and the contact point of the light bulb. If the light bulb lights, the item you are testing is a conductor. An insulator will interrupt the circuit and the bulb will not light.

4. Record the results on the data table.

Item	Your prediction	Is it a conductor or an insulator?

❧ What do all of the conductors have in common?

_____

❧ What do all of the insulators have in common?

_____

❧ What rule can you come up with to help identify items that are conductors and which are insulators?

_____

Make Your Own Light bulb

Gearing Up

Pass some lamp bulbs around the classroom. Have the students study the filament and other inner workings. Pass around a burned-out bulb. Call students' attention to the broken filament. Compare that to the complete circuit they have been exploring in other lessons. Have students observe the glowing filament in a flashlight bulb that is lit.

Process Skills Used
- making a model
- communicating
- observing

Guided Discovery

Background for the teacher:

When electricity flows through the filament of an incandescent bulb, the filament gets hot. The heat energizes the atoms of the filament. These atoms give additional energy in the form of light. To identify the glowing filament up close, use a battery and a flashlight bulb.

Materials needed for each group:

a glass jar

modeling clay

two 30 cm wires with the ends stripped

10 cm nichrome wire (find in broken hair dryers or toasters or in a wire catalog from an electrical store)

two 3-inch (7.5-cm) nails

12-volt lantern battery

Directions for the activity:

Students follow the directions on page **29** to make a homemade light bulb. They are creating a complete circuit with the nichrome wire at the center. The nichrome wire provides the light. If the filament does not light in 15 seconds, have students check all the connections.

Responding to Discovery

Discuss how long it took for the filament to produce light. Discuss how you could make the light burn brighter. Compare the parts of the homemade bulb to a lamp bulb.

Applications and Extensions

Design a switch to turn the bulb on and off.

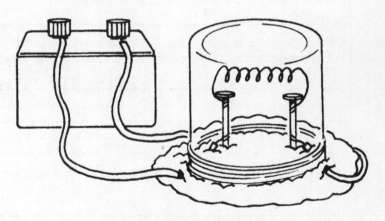

Real-World Applications
- Research Edison's original light bulb.
- Show how most homes and buildings use a variety of forms of light, including incandescent, fluorescent, and neon.

0-7682-3374-7 *Inquiry Science*

Name _____

Make Your Own Light Bulb

Big Question: What part of a bulb produces the light?

🔎 Gather materials and make a homemade light bulb.

1. Make a ball with the clay and flatten it so it is slightly larger than the mouth of the glass jar.

2. Tightly wrap the nichrome wire around the nail so that the coils are not touching each other. Leave 2.5 cm of wire loose on each end to make the filament.

3. Slide the filament wire off of the nail. Twist the loose ends around the heads of the nails.

4. Stick the nails in the modeling clay. Secure one exposed end of each longer, insulated wire to the two nails.

5. Place the jar over the nails and wires so that the free ends of longer wires trail outside the jar. Secure the jar in the modeling clay.

6. Tape the other bare ends of the wires to the battery ends.

🔎 Draw your light bulb.

🔎 How long did it take for the filament to produce light? _____

🔎 How could you make the light burn brighter? _____

🔎 Which part of a light bulb produces the light? _____

🔎 Explain how your setup works to produce light. _____

_____

0-7682-3374-7 *Inquiry Science*

Static Electricity and Bubbles

Gearing Up

Ask the students to recall a time when they walked across a carpeted floor and received a shock by touching something? This is an example of static electricity. (Notice that if you touch the object again, you will not receive a second shock.) Ask two students to hold the four corners of a piece of plastic wrap. Have another student wipe the plastic with a tissue or wool cloth. Have the two students turn the plastic wrap over on top of a pile of small ripped pieces of paper. Observe what happens.

Process Skills Used

- drawing conclusions
- recording data
- collecting data
- forming a hypothesis

Guided Discovery

Background for the teacher:

Static electricity occurs when an electric charge builds up on the surface of an object. When certain objects are rubbed together in a cool, dry environment, there is a transfer of electrons, or negative charges. In this discovery, the balloon picks up electrons and becomes negatively charged with static electricity.

Materials for each pair or group:

bubble solution and a wand (can be shared)

balloon

Directions for the activity:

Teacher tip: This might be a good outdoor activity.

One member of the group blows up the balloon and ties it closed. Have one student blow bubbles into the air toward the balloon. Students observe what happens. Next, one student should rub the balloon back and forth on his/her head five times. Then have a student blow bubbles into the air toward the balloon. Students observe what happens.

Responding to Discovery

Discuss what happened when the balloon was rubbed on the student's head. How did the bubbles act differently after the rubbing? Discuss how long the balloon held the charge that attracted the bubbles.

Applications and Extensions

Take a charged balloon and hold it against the wall. Let it go and see what happens.

Real-World Applications

Research how some people believe that static electricity may have been the cause of the explosion of the Hindenburg while it was docking in New Jersey.

0-7682-3374-7 *Inquiry Science*

Name _____

Static Electricity and Bubbles

- How do bubbles act around static electricity? _____

- Blow up a balloon and tie it closed. Blow bubbles in the air and hold up the balloon. Draw what you observe.

- Using the same balloon, rub it back and forth on the top of your head five times. Blow bubbles in the air again and hold the balloon nearby. Draw what you observe.

- What do you think caused the bubbles to act like they did the second time?

_____

- What happens when you rub the balloon again and hold it over some small bits of paper?

_____

- What happens when you rub the balloon again and hold it against the wall?

_____

- Touch the surface of the balloon with your hand and let go. Record what happens to the balloon on the wall.

_____

- What happens when you rub the balloon on a different part of your body?

_____

- Try rubbing the balloon more than five times. Record your observations.

_____

0-7682-3374-7 *Inquiry Science*

Make Your Own Lightning

Gearing Up

Demonstrate static electricity. Comb your hair with a plastic comb. Hold the comb over a pile of small ripped paper pieces. Ask the students to observe and explain what happens.

> ### Process Skills Used
> - observing
> - recording data
> - simulating
> - following directions
> - calculating

Guided Discovery

Background for the teacher:

Lightning is a form of static electricity. In a storm cloud, moving air causes tiny water droplets and ice to rub together so they become charged with static electricity. The positive electrical charges float to the top of the cloud and the negative charges stay near the bottom of the cloud. This separation of electrical charges is very unstable. Lightning connects the negative charges in the cloud with the positive charges on the ground.

Materials for the demonstration:

A large iron or steel pot (not aluminum) with a plastic handle

rubber gloves

iron or steel fork

plastic sheet

Directions for the activity:

You will simulate lightning in this demonstration. Tape a plastic sheet to a tabletop. Put on rubber gloves and hold the pot by its insulated handle. Rub the pan vigorously back and forth on the plastic sheet. Do not touch the pan.

Holding the fork firmly in one hand and the pot in the other, bring the prongs slowly near the rim of the pot. When the gap between the pot and fork is small, a tiny spark should jump across. (Darken the room to see the spark more clearly.)

Responding to Discovery

Discuss the conditions that created the spark. Ask the students to think of how the pot and fork are like the cloud and the earth in a storm.

Applications and Extensions

Explain why lightning has a sound (thunder). Talk about thunderstorm safety. Calculate the distance of lightning in seconds and miles. A 5-second difference between the lightning flash and the thunder means the lightning struck 1 mile (1.6 km) away. For each additional 5 seconds, the strike is another mile away.

> ### Real-World Applications
> Discuss how you get carpet shocks.

0-7682-3374-7 Inquiry Science

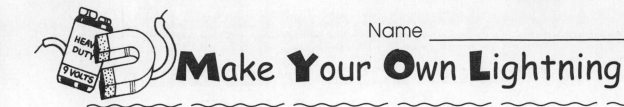

Name _____

Make Your Own Lightning

• Draw what happened when the comb approached the paper pieces.

• Explain what happened when the fork nearly touched the pan.

_____

_____

_____

• Draw a picture of the fork and pan.

• What are some ways that you can stay safe during a thunderstorm?

_____

_____

_____

_____

_____

• How many miles away is the lightning if the thunder comes the following number of seconds behind the lightning?

5 seconds = _____ mile(s)

10 seconds = _____ mile(s)

15 seconds = _____ mile(s)

20 seconds = _____ mile(s)

25 seconds = _____ mile(s)

30 seconds = _____ mile(s)

0-7682-3374-7 Inquiry Science

Performance-Based Assessment

3 = Exceeds expectations
2 = Consistently meets expectations
1 = Below expectations

Student Names

Lesson Investigation Discovery									
Lesson 1: Magnetic Attraction									
Lesson 2: Making a Compass									
Lesson 3: Mapping a Magnet									
Lesson 4: Magnetizing Metals									
Lesson 5: Magnetic Fields									
Lesson 6: Are All Metals Magnetic?									
Lesson 7: Is There Really Iron in Cereals?									
Lesson 8: Exploring Electromagnets									
Lesson 9: Recycled Battery Holder									
Lesson 10: Flashing the Light									
Lesson 11: Conductors and Insulators									
Lesson 12: Make Your Own Light Bulb									
Lesson 13: Static Electricity and Bubbles									
Lesson 14: Make Your Own Lightening									

Specific Lesson Skills									
Can make a reasonable hypothesis.									
Can identify the poles of a magnet.									
Can make detailed observations.									
Can propose an explanation.									
Can follow directions.									
Shows safe lab habits.									
Works well within a small group or class.									
Participates in discussions.									
Can record data gathered from investigations.									
Can classify data in meaningful categories.									
Can communicate through writing and/or drawing.									
Can apply what is learned to real-world situations.									

0-7682-3374-7 *Inquiry Science*

Invertebrates

0-7682-3374-7 *Inquiry Science*

Earthworm Exploration

Gearing Up

Get students thinking about earthworms by generating a three-column KWL chart. Ask students what they know (K) about earthworms. On a piece of chart paper, list all their responses (accurate or not). Then in the second column, list what the students want (W) to know about earthworms. Leave the third column empty. Later, you will record what the students say they have learned (L) about earthworms.

Process Skills Used

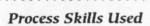

- observing
- measuring
- comparing
- communicating

Guided Discovery

Background information for the teacher:
Earthworms belong to a group of animals called *annelids*. The word *annelid* means "ringed." The worm's body is divided into ringlike segments called *annuli*. Each segment has eight tiny bristles, called *setae*. The worm uses the *setae* to help it move through the earth.

The earthworm moves using two types of muscles. By tightening the muscles that circle each segment, the earthworm stretches out and gets skinnier. By contracting the long muscles that run down the length of the worm, the earthworm becomes shorter and fatter.

The top side of an earthworm is rounded and cylindrical while its underside is flat and lighter in color.

Materials needed for each student:
earthworm*
one 12-oz. (350 ml) clear plastic cup filled with soil
magnifying glass
ruler
triple-beam balance scale

Directions for the activity:
Using page 37 as a guide, students will explore, observe, and draw their earthworm. Note: Earthworms must be kept moist at all times or they will die.

*Earthworms are available from bait shops or pet stores.

Responding to Discovery

Have students pair up and compare and discuss their activity sheets. On a separate sheet of paper, have students create a graphic organizer to visually show the similarities and differences between their worms.

Use cheesecloth to cover the worms in the cups of moist soil and store overnight in a cool, dry place.

Applications and Extensions

- Have students put two worms in the same cup and observe.
- Challenge the students to dig for worms in their yards. Have them predict where they will find the most worms. Discuss what they found and ask them to propose explanations.
- Assign research to find the names of other types of worms.

Real-World Applications
- Why do earthworms come out of the ground when it rains?

0-7682-3374-7 *Inquiry Science*

Name _____

Earthworm Exploration

In this discovery, you will be observing and drawing your earthworm.

• Use a magnifying glass to observe the earthworm. Record five observations.

_____

_____

_____

_____

• Contrast the earthworm to the human body. What features are different?

_____

_____

• Compare and contrast the top side of the earthworm to its underside.

_____

_____

• Measure your earthworm.

Length (take three measurements) _____ cm _____ cm _____ cm

Width at its widest point _____ mm

Find the mass of your earthworm _____ grams

• Gently touch your earthworm with a wet finger. Describe how it feels.

_____

_____

• Name something that feels similar to the skin of your earthworm. _____

• Draw a detailed picture of your entire earthworm in the large box. In the smaller box, draw an enlarged close-up section of any part of the earthworm.

0-7682-3374-7 *Inquiry Science*

Earthworm Environments

Gearing Up

Review the information gathered in the previous lesson on the KWL chart. Ask the students what they have learned so far. Record their responses in the L column. Allow students to observe their earthworms for 5 minutes.

Process Skills Used
- observing
- communicating
- comparing
- forming hypotheses

Guided Discovery

Background information for the teacher:
Earthworms have neither ears nor eyes. They use their skin to sense light and darkness, sound, moisture or lack of moisture, textures, and their environment in general. Earthworms are nocturnal animals and prefer darkness to light. They prefer dampness to dryness and smooth surfaces as opposed to rough ones.

Materials needed for each group:
earthworm for each student
three paper towels
black construction paper
flashlight
8" x 10" (20 cm x 25 cm) piece of fine mesh screen with edges taped
white sheet of paper

Directions for the activity:
In this lesson, students will be exploring different environments and conditions to see how the earthworms respond. Have students follow the directions on page 39 and complete the sheet.

Responding to Discovery

Students should analyze their results and draw conclusions. For example, if Reba's worm chose the wet paper towel 3 out of 5 times, she can conclude that her earthworm prefers a wet environment. Discuss the results from individual experiments.

On a large sheet of paper or the chalkboard, make a bar graph. Students should fill in their individual data on the class graph.

Number of Earthworms | Wet Dry Rough Smooth Dark Light

Discuss the graph data. Challenge students to explain, find patterns, and come to conclusions regarding earthworms and their environments.

Use cheesecloth to cover the worms in the cups of moist soil and store overnight in a cool, dry place.

Applications and Extensions

Students can design and carry out their own experiments. (Students will need teacher approval in order to insure that the experiment will not be harmful to the earthworm.) Encourage experiments that explore how earthworms respond to touch, food preferences, sounds, and textures.

Real-World Applications
- Compare earthworm preferences to those of other animals.
- How do deaf or blind people sense their environments?

0-7682-3374-7 *Inquiry Science*

Name _____

Earthworm Environments

In the following experiments, you will discover which environments or conditions your earthworm prefers.

Conduct five trials for each experiment so that you may have the most accurate conclusions.

Do earthworms prefer light or dark?

Materials: flashlight, black paper

Directions:
Fold the black construction paper lengthwise and set it on the table so it resembles a tent.
Standing next to the tent, hold the flashlight 7 inches (18 cm) from the table top.
Shine the light down on one side of the tent. Place the earthworm in the flashlight beam. Wait a few minutes and observe the earthworm.
Record your results in the chart.
Repeat the experiment 4 more times.

Test Number	1	2	3	4	5
Prefers light area					
Prefers dark area					

Do earthworms prefer rough or smooth surfaces?

Materials: white paper, mesh screen

Directions:
Overlapping slightly, place the screen next to the paper. Put the earthworm where the screen meets the paper. Observe the earthworm for a few minutes. Record your results.
Repeat the experiment 4 more times.

Test Number	1	2	3	4	5
Prefers mesh screen					
Prefers white paper					

Do earthworms prefer a moist or dry environment?

Materials: a wet and a dry paper towel

Directions:
Place the two paper towels next to each other and put your earthworm where the two paper towels meet. Observe the earthworm.
Record your results in the chart. Repeat the experiment 4 more times.

Test Number	1	2	3	4	5
Prefers wet towel					
Prefers dry towel					

Based on the above experiments, I conclude that earthworms prefer _____

_____

My evidence is _____

_____

0-7682-3374-7 *Inquiry Science*

Home, Sweet Home

Gearing Up

Write the word *habitat* on the board and ask students to explain what a habitat is. Make sure all students understand the meaning of habitat. Discuss habitats of familiar animals. Ask each student to draw the habitat they predict that an earthworm has. In the drawing, they should include its food and any types of predators they believe it may have.

> ### Process Skills Used
> - observing
> - making a model
> - communicating

Guided Discovery

Background information for the teacher:
Earthworms live underground where the soil is cool, dark, and damp. As earthworms burrow into the soil and make tunnels, they mix up the soil layers and decompose dead organic matter, thus fertilizing the soil. Because earthworms are continuously tunneling below the surface, they not only aerate the soil, but also bring rich soil to the surface. A sign of healthy soil is that it contains many earthworms.

Although earthworms must be kept damp, they will die if they become too wet. Earthworms breathe through their skin. They get oxygen from the air holes in dirt around them. If those air holes fill with water, the earthworms will drown. When it rains, earthworms come to the surface in an attempt of avoid drowning.

Materials needed for each student:
earthworm
large, clear glass jar (1 gallon (4 liter) size)
empty soup can
potting soil
sand or gravel
decayed leaves or plant material
black construction paper

> Earthworm care: Do not keep the worms more than two weeks. Earthworm homes should be kept in a cool, dark place in the classroom. Every three days, students should lightly mist their earthworm homes with water.

Directions for the activity:
Using page 41 as a guide, students will construct individual earthworm homes.

Responding to Discovery

Complete the KWL chart by discussing what students have learned about earthworms. Discuss any misconceptions from the first day, as well.

Applications and Extensions

- Have students create a graphic organizer or chart comparing and contrasting the habitats of two animals (such as moles and ants, bees and squirrels, or birds and worms). Information can be based on their prior knowledge or research.

- Have students create mini books to share what they have learned about earthworms.

> ### Real-World Applications
> - What animals share habitats?
> - Why do farmers love worms?
> - Where is the best place to release the earthworms so they can survive?

0-7682-3374-7 *Inquiry Science*

Name _____

Home, Sweet Home

In this activity, you will create a habitat for your earthworm and observe the changes over one to two weeks.

Directions:

🐛 Pour 1 inch (2½ cm) of potting soil in the bottom of the jar.

🐛 Place soup can with open end down and closed end up in the middle of the jar. Add potting soil to the top of the tin can.

🐛 Add one inch of sand or gravel. Add ¼ inch (½ cm) of decayed leaves or other plant material.

🐛 Put your earthworm in the jar.

🐛 In the box below, draw a picture of your earthworm home. Cover the outside of the jar with black construction paper.

🐛 After one week, remove the construction paper. Draw your changed earthworm home.

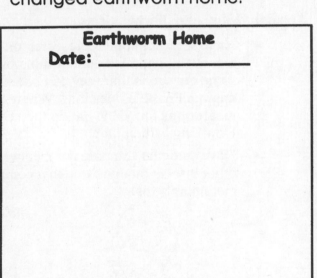

Earthworm Home Date: _____	**Earthworm Home (1 week later)** Date: _____

How has your earthworm home changed in the past week?
Write your observations below.

_____

_____

_____

0-7682-3374-7 *Inquiry Science*

Marvelous Mealworms

Gearing Up

Pass out a mealworm larva to each group of four students. Ask the groups to come to a concensus about what type of animal it is. Have each group tell the class its decision along with supporting arguments.

Tell the student that the animal is a mealworm larva and pass out magnifying glasses. Have each group create a Venn diagram comparing the physical characteristics of a mealworm larva and an earthworm.

Process Skills Used
- observing
- measuring
- comparing
- questioning

Mealworm care: Store in a deep, glass container a quarter full of oatmeal. Add and replace small pieces of apples or potatoes every day. Store uncovered in a cool, dark place.

Directions for the activity:
Using page 43 as a guide, students will draw and make observations of three of the four stages of the mealworm life cycle.

Responding to Discovery

Create a chart on the chalkboard with the following headings: Larva, Pupa, Adult. Record the students' observations. Discuss their findings.

Guided Discovery

Background information for the teacher:
Mealworms are actually the larval stage of the grain beetle. This insect goes through a complete metamorphosis. Its life cycle begins with tiny, white eggs that are approximately 1 mm in length. In one to two weeks, these eggs hatch into larvae (mealworms). It is at this stage that they begin to eat. The larvae feed on grains such as oatmeal and flour. After two to three weeks, and after shedding its skin many times, it enters the pupal stage. The pupa is a smaller and fatter mealworm shaped like a beetle. After two to three weeks, the pupa turns into a grain beetle, the final stage of the metamorphosis.

Materials needed for each student:
one mealworm larva, pupa, and adult
magnifying glass
colored pencils
ruler

Applications and Extensions

- Have students conduct research on the mealworm or grain beetle. Brainstorm some questions that they can attempt to answer. Possible questions: Where are mealworms found? What do they eat? How long is their life?

- Have students compare the mealworm to other insects that go through a complete metamorphosis.

Real-World Applications
- How can you keep insects out of your flour at home?
- pests vs. helpful insects

0-7682-3374-7 *Inquiry Science*

Name _____

Marvelous Mealworms

Observe the three stages of the life cycle of the mealworm.
Draw what you see through the magnifying glass.

Drawing of larva:

Larva Observations:

color:_____

length: _____

number of legs: _____

number of antennae: _____

other observations: _____

_____

_____

Drawing of pupa:

Pupa Observations:

color:_____

length: _____

other observations: _____

_____

_____

Drawing of adult:

Adult Observations:

color:_____

length: _____

other observations: _____

_____

_____

0-7682-3374-7 *Inquiry Science*

Mealworm Environments

aring Up

Allow the students several minutes to observe the mealworms and ask questions. Discuss what they learned in the previous lesson.

> ### Process Skills Used
> * observing
> * comparing
> * questioning

ided Discovery

Background information for the teacher:
Mealworms prefer damp and dark environments. It is likely that the mealworms have burrowed into the potatoes in their jars. They gain both nutrients and moisture from the potatoes.

Materials needed for each student:
one mealworm larva
two paper towels
five dried beans
small cubes of a fresh potato
wax paper
plastic cup half full of oatmeal

Directions for the activity:
Using page 45 as a guide, students will conduct three experiments to determine the best mealworm environment. They will test whether mealworms prefer potatoes or beans, a wet environment over a dry one, and darkness or light.

sponding to Discovery

Students should analyze their results and draw conclusions. For example, if Eric's mealworm chose the potato 3 out of 5 times, he can conclude that his mealworm prefers

potatoes to beans. Discuss the results from individual experiments.

On a large sheet of paper or the chalkboard, make a bar graph. Students should fill in their individual data on the class graph.

Number of Mealworms

| Wet | Dry | Rough | Smooth | Dark | Light |

Discuss the graph data. Challenge students to explain, find patterns, and come to conclusions regarding mealworms and their environments.

Applications and Extensions

Students can design and carry out their own experiments. (Students will need teacher approval in order to insure that the experiment will not be harmful to the mealworm.) Encourage experiments that explore how much mealworms eat in a week, food preferences, changes over time, and response to sound and temperature.

> ### Real-World Applications
> * stages of growth in humans
> * food web

0-7682-3374-7 *Inquiry Science*

Name _____

Mealworm Environments

In the following experiments, you will discover which environment or conditions your mealworm prefers.

Conduct five trials for each experiment so that you may have the most accurate conclusions.

Do mealworms prefer light or dark?

Materials: plastic cup half filled with oatmeal

Test Number	1	2	3	4	5
Prefers light area					
Prefers dark area					

Directions:
Put the mealworm on top of the oatmeal.
For each trial, observe your mealworm for four minutes.
If it burrows, it probably prefers dark.
Record your results. Repeat the experiment 4 more times.

Do mealworms prefer potatoes to beans?

Materials: potato, dried beans, wax paper

Test Number	1	2	3	4	5
Prefers potatoes					
Prefers beans					

Directions:
Place the mealworm in the middle of a sheet of wax paper with beans on one side and potato cubes on the other. The mealworm needs to be three inches (8 cm) away from each of them. For each trial, observe your mealworm for four minutes. Record the results in the chart. Repeat the experiment 4 more times.

Do mealworms prefer a moist or dry environment?

Materials: a wet and a dry paper towel

Test Number	1	2	3	4	5
Prefers wet towel					
Prefers dry towel					

Directions:
Place the two paper towels next to each other and put the mealworm where the two paper towels meet. Observe where the mealworm goes. Record where the mealworm stays. Repeat the experiment 4 more times.

Based on the above experiments, I conclude that mealworms prefer _____

_____ .

My evidence is _____

_____ .

0-7682-3374-7 *Inquiry Science*

Lovely Ladybugs

Gearing Up

Introduce or review the meaning of *symmetry*. Brainstorm a list of things that display symmetry, such as the human face, our bodies, butterflies, some alphabet letters, and a square. Have students observe ladybugs to determine whether they are symmetrical.

Ladybugs can be found outdoors in the spring or ordered through Insect Lore at 1-805-746-6047.

Directions for the activity:
Using page 47 as a guide, students will observe, draw, and measure their ladybugs.
Using page 47 as a guide, students will observe, draw, and measure their ladybugs.

Process Skills Used
- observing
- measuring
- communicating

Responding to Discovery

On a large sheet of paper, create a web with spokes around the word *ladybug*. Have students add to the web their observations, physical descriptions, and other discoveries about ladybugs.

Have students create a Venn diagram comparing the ladybug to the mealworm.

Guided Discovery

Background information for the teacher:
Ladybugs are beetles. They are also called ladybird beetles. Ladybugs are helpful to farmers and gardeners because they eat harmful pests such as aphids.

Ladybugs are insects with six legs attached to their thorax. Their shells are made up of two front wings. These wings protect the transparent hind wings. As with all insects, the ladybug has antennae and compound eyes. The ladybug has two sets of jaws and pinchers for grasping its prey. Like the mealworm, ladybugs undergo a complete metamorphosis.

Store ladybugs in an aquarium covered with a screen. Provide aphids and raisins for the ladybugs to eat.

Materials needed for each student:
one ladybug*
magnifying glass
metric ruler
colored pencils

Applications and Extensions

Read *The Grouchy Ladybug* by Eric Carle. To give students an understanding of how insects see through compound eyes, purchase a Fly's Eye or another similar viewer that is readily found in toy stores or museum gift shops.

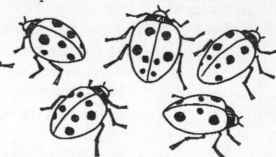

Real-World Applications
- Pros and cons of pesticides
- What are some beneficial insects?

0-7682-3374-7 *Inquiry Science*

Name _____

Lovely Ladybugs

In the following activity, you will observe, measure, and draw your ladybug.

Using your magnifying glass, carefully observe your ladybug's top side.

- Background color _____
- Number of spots _____
- Length of ladybug _____ mm
- Width of ladybug _____ mm
- Number of eyes _____
- Number of jaws _____
- Number of pinchers _____
- Other observations _____

_____

_____

_____

Top View of Ladybug

Gently turn your ladybug over onto its back. Using your magnifying glass, carefuly observe the underside of your ladybug.

- Body color _____
- Number of legs _____
- Length of ladybug leg _____ mm
- Number of segments on abdomen _____
- Other observations _____

_____

_____

_____

Underneath View of Ladybug

0-7682-3374-7 *Inquiry Science*

Beautiful Butterflies

Gearing Up

Ask the class "How do butterflies form?" They should attempt to answer the question based on their prior knowledge. Record their answers on chart paper to be reviewed later.

Conduct this month-long activity in the mid to late spring so the butterflies can be released outside at the end. Purchase larvae from Carolina Biological Supply Company at (336) 584-0381.

Process Skills Used
- observing
- comparing
- communicating

Guided Discovery

Background information for the teacher:
Butterflies live throughout the world except where it is very cold. In the winter, some butterflies will migrate to warmer places. North America alone has more than 700 species of butterflies. Like the ladybug and the mealworm, butterflies also undergo a complete metamorphosis. In addition to a butterfly's three body parts, four wings, six legs, and two antennae, they also have palps. These palps can be found below the eyes. They function as sensing organs and shield the butterfly's tongue. Butterflies use their tubelike tongues to sip the nectar from flowers.

The delicate butterfly larvae and pupae should not be handled.

Materials needed for each group:
butterfly larvae
clear jar with a screen cover
magnifying glasses
food (information will arrive with larvae)
bottle caps filled with water
individual sections from the bottom of a
    cardboard egg carton

Directions for the activity:
Prepare the habitat for the butterfly larvae. It must have food, ventilation, and moisture. Caterpillars need a drier environment than the pupae.

On the bottom of the jar (or small aquarium), place egg carton sections and bottle caps of water. Lean a twig against the side of the jar. Place the larvae and their food in the jar. Students will observe the larvae and record observations on page 49.

Have each student target one larva for observation through its life cycle. Every few days, students write observations on page 49.

Responding to Discovery

As students keep track of the changes in the jar, have them share their observations and predictions with the class. Encourage the students to ask questions and help them find answers to their questions.

Applications and Extensions

Have students research and report on a different species of butterfly.

Real-World Applications
- life cycles
- respect for nature

Name _____

Beautiful Butterflies

Over the next 3–4 weeks, observe the growth and change of your butterfly. In the space below, draw the different stages. Date and make observations 2–3 times per week.

Larva (Caterpillar)

Date	Observations

Pupa (Chrysalis)

Date	Observations

Adult (Butterfly)

Date	Observations

0-7682-3374-7 *Inquiry Science*

Amazing Ants

Gearing Up

Find out what students already know about ants by asking them to name as many ants as they can think of. (There are about 20,000 different species of ants.) Start a word web with the word "Ants" in the center and the types students can name around the center. Add facts that students can recall under each type.

Then, pair students up to use a variety of resource books and discover more types of ants and interesting facts. After 20 minutes of research, return to a whole class group and complete the web with student research.

Process Skills Used
- observing
- measuring
- communicating

Guided Discovery

Background information for the teacher:
Ants live in large groups called colonies. Each colony has at least one queen. The queen's responsibility is to lay eggs. She can lay thousands of eggs in her lifetime. The male ant's responsibility is to mate with the queen. The female ants are the workers in the ant colony.

Ants, like other insects, have three body parts (head, thorax, and abdomen). They have six legs and two antennae. Ants use their antennae as sensors. Their antennae help them to sense the environment, find food, and communicate with each other. Some ants can carry up to 50 times their own weight!

Materials needed for each group:
an active anthill
(not fire or harvester ants which bite)
meter stick   stopwatch
sugar   salt
unsweetened drink mix
unsalted sunflower seeds out of the shell
4" x 6" (10 cm x 15 cm) index cards

Directions for the activity:
Send groups out to the playground to observe anthills. Using page **51 as a guide**, students will make observations, answer questions, and conduct a food preference experiment.

Responding to Discovery

Students will discuss findings with the class. Create a class chart to compare data collected about ant food preferences. Have students infer generalizations based on the commmon evidence. Discuss how ants might respond to foods found in students lunches.

Applications and Extensions

Create a T-chart showing how ants are helpful and harmful.

helpful | harmful

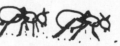

Real-World Applications
- How do people use nonverbal communication?

0-7682-3374-7 *Inquiry Science*

Name _____

Amazing Ants

Observe an anthill. You will need a stopwatch, meter stick, a pencil, and this paper.

Choose an interesting ant to watch and make the following observations:

- Is your ant traveling away from the anthill or towards it? _____

- Is your ant carrying anything? _____ If so, what? _____

- Esimate the length of your ant. _____

- Using your meter stick as a guide, time how long it takes your ant to travel a meter. _____

Food Preference Experiment:

Materials: sugar, unsweetened drink mix, salt, unsalted sunflower seeds, 2 large index cards

Directions:

- Place the index cards side by side four ft. (1¼ m) away from anthill. On half of the first index card, pour a small pile of sugar. On the other half, pour a small pile of sunflower seeds. On half of the second index card, pour a small pile of salt. On the other half, pour a small pile of unsweetened drink mix.

- On the chart below, record your predictions about ant preferences.

- Observe the ants for fifteen to twenty minutes and record your observations.

Foods	Predictions	Observations
Sugar		
Sunflower Seeds		
Salt		
Unsweetened Drink Mix		

0-7682-3374-7 *Inquiry Science*

Awesome Ant Farms

Gearing Up

As a class, have students make general observations about the physical features of an anthill. Ask students to make predictions based upon prior knowledge of what lies beneath an anthill. Most students will be able to explain that ants live and work in tunnels that they dig beneath the soil. Students should be able to compare this type of home to an earthworm's home.

> ### Process Skills Used
> - making a model
> - observing
> - communicating

Guided Discovery

In this lesson, the students will create a mini ant farm. There are two ways to get ants:

Option 1: Ants may be gathered as a class by carefully digging into an anthill. Students should spread out large plastic garbage bags to put the dirt and ants onto. Ants can be collected from the dirt on the bag and put into plastic resealable bags with tiny holes in the bags. If students carefully sift through the dirt they may also find the eggs, larvae and pupae. Students should try to find a queen from the colony for their ant farm as well. While ants can build their homes and live without a queen, they will live much longer with her in the colony.

Option 2: If you do not want to go to the trouble of gathering ants, ants may also be purchased from science catalogs that sell commercially made ant farms or from science supply houses.

Materials needed for each group:

1 one-gallon (4 liter) glass jar
a piece of cheesecloth or nylon
rubber bands
dirt
sand
decayed plan material
large tin can
small sponge
cookie and cereal crumbs
black construction paper
ants in various stages of life (egg, larva, pupa, adult)

Directions for the activity:

Using the directions on the student page, students will work in groups of 4–6 to construct an ant farm.

Responding to Discovery

Have students share their observations of the ant farms. They can discuss the behaviors of the ants in their new homes. Do the ants act the same in the different ant farms? Have students compare ant farms.

> ### Real-World Applications
> - How do you make yourself at home in a new place?

0-7682-3374-7 *Inquiry Science*

Name _____

Awesome Ant Farms

Follow the directions and use the materials provided to construct an awesome ant farm with your group.

- Fill the bottom of a large glass jar (1 gallon size) with a mixture of dirt and sand.

- Place an open aluminum can upside down in the jar.

- Fill the jar with a mixture of dirt, sand, and decayed plant material. Leave 5" (13 cm) of open space at the top of the jar.

- Place a damp sponge on top of the dirt in the jar. Sprinkle cookie and cereal crumbs on the sponge.

- Collect ants from a single location and put them in the ant farm.

- Poke holes in the lid and cover the jar.

- When you are not making observations, cover the outside of the jar with black construction paper.

- Release the ants in their original location after one week.

Draw the Ant Farm.

Date: _____

Draw the Ant Farm four days later.

Date: _____

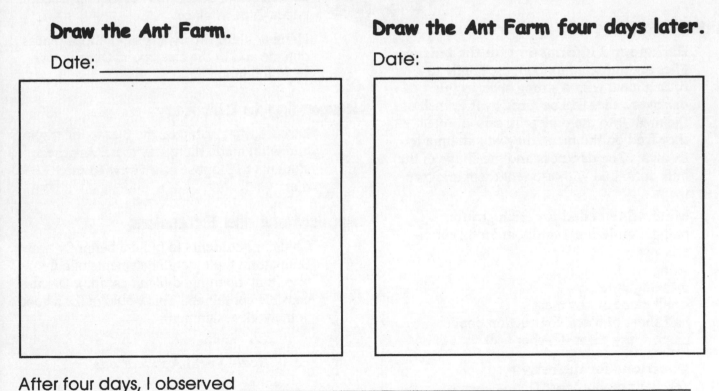

After four days, I observed _____

_____.

0-7682-3374-7 *Inquiry Science*

Build a Better Fly Trap

Gearing Up

As an introduction to this lesson, have students complete the anticipation guide on page 55. First have students read the statements on the top of the page. To the left of the statements, they write either true or false. Then, students read the informational text about flies at the bottom of the page. After reading, they read the statements on the top of page 55 again. This time they write true or false to the right of the statements. Compare their predictions from the *before reading* column to the *after reading* column.

> *Process Skills Used*
> * predicting
> * making a model
> * observing
> * communicating

Guided Discovery

Background information for the teacher:
Flies are attracted to food, especially to rotting meat with a strong odor. In this discovery, flies will be lured by the smell of the meat into the dark milk carton. After they feed on the meat, they will attempt to fly away. The darkness and the shape of the milk container will disorient them and trap them.

Materials needed for each group:
half-gallon (2 liter) cardboard milk carton
scissors
string
masking tape
small piece of raw meat
half sheet of black contruction paper
black spray paint (teacher use)

Directions for the activity:
Teacher preparations: The day before, cut the bottom off the cardboard cartons. Spray the insides of the cartons with black paint and allow them to dry overnight in a well ventilated place.

Student directions: Tie a small piece of meat on a string. Poke a small hole in the top of the carton and thread the string up through the hole so the meat hangs just inside the carton near the top. Tape the other end of the string to the outside of the container. Cover the hole with a piece of tape. (Students must wash their hands with soap after handling meat.)

Cut a 1" x 1" (2½ cm x 2½ cm) square at the base of the carton to allow flies in. Cover the bottom of the carton with black construction paper. Tape in place.

Hang or place the fly traps in various places outside and in the classroom. Observe over several hours.

Responding to Discovery

Discuss what attracted the flies to the traps and what made them stay there. Ask the students to propose other ways to catch flies.

Applications and Extensions

Challenge students to build a better fly trap. Brainstorm the essential elements of a fly trap (bait, opening, difficult escape). Discuss possible containers. This would make a good homework assignment.

> *Real-World Applications*
> * bug sprays and flyswatters
> * pests vs helpful insects

0-7682-3374-7 *Inquiry Science*

Build a Better Fly Trap

Complete the anticipation guide and reading selection to learn more about "Fascinating Flies." To begin, fold the bottom of your paper back so you can only see the six statements below.

Read the six statements. Write *T* (true) or *F* (false) in the "Before Reading" column. Then unfold your paper and read the passage about flies. After reading, read the six statements again. This time write *T* or *F* in the "After Reading" column.

Anticipation Guide

Before Reading   **After Reading**

_____   1. A fly is an insect.   _____

_____   2. Flies have been around for about 1,000 years.   _____

_____   3. Flies are not harmful to humans, just annoying.   _____

_____   4. A fly has a head and abdomen, but no thorax.   _____

_____   5. A fly uses its proboscis to sip liquids.   _____

_____   6. Flies undergo a complete metamorphosis.

Fascinating Flies

The fly is an insect with exactly two wings. There are over 100,000 different types of flies. Butterflies are not flies because they have four wings. Flies have been around for 200 million years.

Some flies are helpful and others are harmful. Fruit flies have been useful in heredity experiments. The tachina fly kills gypsy moths which are known to do great damage to plants. Some flies carry diseases. Other flies destroy plants. Mosquitoes are flies that "bite." Some flies are simply a nuisance to people.

A fly's body consists of three parts: the head, the thorax, and the abdomen. It has compound eyes that cover most of its head. The mouth of the fly is called a *proboscis*. The proboscis is shaped like a

funnel and is used to sip liquids, which are a fly's only food.

The adult female fly may lay anywhere from 1–250 eggs, depending on the species. The eggs develop very quickly. They may hatch within 8 hours. The larvae, often resembling worms, eat and grow for a few days. The larvae may eat garbage. The larva turns into a pupa which is the stage before an adult. It changes from its wormlike appearance to a flylike appearance. This may occur in a cocoon or a strong oval case. In 3–6 days, the fly emerges full size with its two wings.

For better or worse, flies have been around for millions of years and will likely be around for millions more.

    0-7682-3374-7 *Inquiry Science*

Crazy Crickets

Gearing Up

Play "Who Am I?" Use the following clues.

- I am an animal.
- I am an insect that can be dark brown or black.
- I undergo an incomplete metamorphosis (young is a miniature version of an adult).
- Toads, snakes, and birds think I am a tasty treat.
- I can be a pest to farmers.
- If I am a female, I have an ovipositor, which is a long tube for laying eggs on the ground.
- If I am a male, I can sing by rubbing my wings together. My songs either attract a mate or challenge other males to fight.
- I can jump up to 2 feet (60 cm). If a 5 ft. (1½ m) human could jump like me, it would be able to jump 120 feet (36 m)!

> *Process Skills Used*
> - observing
> - making a model
> - measuring
> - communicating

Guided Discovery

Materials needed for each student:
one cricket
magnifying glass
metric ruler
small, clear container with holes in the lid
slice of potato
colored pencils

Directions for the activity:
Put the crickets in the refrigerator for an hour before the lesson. This will slow them down for observations. Have the students observe their own crickets and draw a detailed picture. Then, using page 57 as a

guide, the students will measure and look at specific parts of the cricket.

> Crickets can be purchased at pet stores or bait shops.

Responding to Discovery

Discussion questions:

- What do crickets have in common with other insects?
- What physical trait is unique to the cricket?
- How does the cricket move?
- How does the cricket eat?
- What would you like to find out about your cricket?

Applications and Extensions

Students can design and carry out their own experiments. (Students will need teacher approval in order to insure that the experiment will not be harmful to the cricket.) Encourage experiments that explore how crickets respond to touch, food preferences, sounds, and textures.

> *Real-World Applications*
> - Compare crickets to grasshoppers.
> - music

0-7682-3374-7 *Inquiry Science*

Name _____

Crazy Crickets

- At first, your cricket will be cold and slow moving. In the space below, draw, color, and label a detailed picture of your cricket.

- Find and label the following parts: *head, thorax, abdomen, wings, legs, antennae, and cerci* (the two spikey spines that are on the rear portion of the abdomen).

- If your cricket is female, it will have an *ovipositor*, a long, needle-shaped feature that is in between the cerci and on the bottom of the abdomen. If your cricket is a female, draw and label the ovipositor.

- Measure your cricket's body.

    length: _____ cm _____ mm   **width:** _____ mm

- Measure one antenna of your cricket.

    _____ cm _____ mm

- Is the antenna longer, shorter, or the same length as the cricket's

    body? _____

- Observe the cricket's wings. Nymphs do not have wings; adolescent crickets have very small wings; and adult crickets have larger wings.
    Is your cricket a nymph, adolescent, or adult? _____

- Using your magnifying glass, carefully study the delicate and detailed cricket wing.

At this point, your cricket should be warm and more active. Place the cricket in a container with breathing holes and a potato. Study its behavior for five minutes.

Record your observations on the lines below.

_____

_____

_____

    0-7682-3374-7 *Inquiry Science*

Snazzy Snails

Gearing Up

Ask the students what they know about snails. Write their contributions on a large chart to review later.

Process Skills Used
- observing
- measuring
- questioning
- communicating

Guided Discovery

Background information for the teacher:
There are about 40 thousand different types of snails and slugs. Snails have shells that they carry around and use as protection for their soft bodies.

The snail's body consists of a head and a "foot." The head supports one or two pairs of tentacles, two eyes, and a radula (an organ that shreds food and takes it into the snail's mouth). The body, or foot, secretes a slimy substance that makes it easier to move across any surface. Snails are called gastropods, which means "stomach-footed."

Materials needed for each student:
snail
metric ruler
triple-beam balance scale (shared)
black construction paper
magnifying glass
small pieces of orange peel
small pieces of garlic
pepper
small piece of lettuce

Directions for the activity:
Teach the students how to handle the snails with care. Students should wash their hands before and after handling snails. You may provide rubber gloves for students to wear while handling snails.

Allow the students time to observe the snails. Students should observe their physical characteristics and movement for several minutes before you pass out page **59** for formal observations. Encourage questioning. The students will conduct an experiment to find out which foods the snails prefer.

Order your snails from Connecticut Valley Biological Supply Company at 1-800-628-7748. Keep them in an aquarium with a screen top. Line the bottom of the aquarium with rocks and wood pieces. Include a shallow lid with water and food that you change weekly.

Responding to Discovery

Write a half-page summary of what you observed and discovered about the snail. Review the chart from the introduction. Did your observations disprove anything that you thought you knew about snails?

Applications and Extensions

- Have students make mini presentations on different types of snails.

- Have students create snail art: Fill the very bottom of shallow bowls with diluted food coloring. Gently dip the snail's foot into the coloring and place the snail on glossy white paper. Use a number of snails and colors to get different color snail trails.

Real-World Applications
- Why do gardeners dislike slugs?
- shell patterns

0-7682-3374-7 *Inquiry Science*

Name _____

Snazzy Snails

- Place your snail on a clean surface. Use a magnifying glass to observe its appearance and movements. In the box below, draw, color, and label a detailed picture of your snail.

- Find and label the following parts: *shell, breathing hole, eyes, upper tentacles, lower tentacles, and foot.*

- Measure the length of your snail. _____ mm

- Measure one of the tentacles. _____ mm

- Find the mass of your snail. _____ grams

- Gently touch the upper tentacles.

  Record what happens. _____

  _____

- Gently tap the snail shell with your fingernail. Record what happens.

  _____

- Place your snail on a piece of black paper. Time it for one minute and measure the wet trail it leaves. How far does your snail travel in one minute? _____ mm

Snail Preferences Experiment

- Place the snail on a clean surface. Place the four foods around the snail—each 2 cm away. Record your observations over several minutes.

Food	Observations
Lettuce	
Pepper	
Orange Peel	
Garlic	

Published by Frank Schaffer Publications. Copyright protected.

0-7682-3374-7 *Inquiry Science*

Bashful Brine Shrimp

Gearing Up

Pass out a vial of brine shrimp eggs to each student or pair of students. Ask the students to draw a picture to predict what the animals that hatch will look like. Save the pictures for comparison to the actual.

> *Process Skills Used*
> - observing
> - comparing
> - questioning

Guided Discovery

Background information for the teacher:
Brine shrimp undergo an incomplete metamorphosis (young looks like a miniature adult). They develop from egg to adult in about one month. When fully grown, they may reach 1/2" (1 cm) in length with 10 or more pairs of limbs that help them eat and move through the water.

Materials needed for each student:
brine shrimp kit (purchase at a pet store)
magnifying glass

Directions for the activity:
Follow the directions on the kit to start the brine shrimp. The students will use their magnifying glasses to observe the progress of the development over the next 15–30 days. Every fifth day, the students should record their observations on page 61.

Responding to Discovery

Set up an experiment in which you control variables while testing five different environments for the brine shrimp. Design a graphic organizer for recording daily observations of the shrimp in each environment.

Add brine shrimp and given amounts of salt to 1 cup (240 ml) water at 70° F (21° C). Assign responsibility for the following different environments to student groups:

1. no salt
2. 1 teaspoon salt (5 ml)
3. 7 teaspoons salt (35 ml)
4. 14 teaspoons salt (70 ml)
5. 21 teaspoons salt (104 ml)

Applications and Extensions

Have students brainstorm and research a list of animals that are oviparous (come from eggs).

Discuss how changes in environment can affect behavior and development of animals and people.

> *Real-World Applications*
> - Where do brine shrimp live?
> - salt-water animals

0-7682-3374-7 *Inquiry Science*

Name _____

Bashful Brine Shrimp

> You will draw and make observations on the development of your brine shrimp eggs.

Directions:

Following the instructions your teacher gives you, make a salt water solution in which your brine shrimp will grow and develop. Use a magnifying glass to observe the brine shrimp. Every five days, draw and write about what you observe.

Brine Shrimp Observations and Illustrations

Day 5:

Day 10:

Day 15:

Day 20:

Day 25:

Day 30:

0-7682-3374-7 *Inquiry Science*

Performance-Based Assessment

3 = Exceeds expectations
2 = Consistently meets expectations
1 = Below expectations

Student Names

Lesson Investigation Discovery											
Lesson 1: Earthworm Exploration											
Lesson 2: Earthworm Environments											
Lesson 3: Home, Sweet Home											
Lesson 4: Marvelous Mealworms											
Lesson 5: Mealworm Environments											
Lesson 6: Lovely Ladybugs											
Lesson 7: Beautiful Butterflies											
Lesson 8: Amazing Ants											
Lesson 9: Awesome Ant Farms											
Lesson 10: Build a Better Fly Trap											
Lesson 11: Crazy Crickets											
Lesson 12: Snazzy Snails											
Lesson 13: Bashful Brine Shrimp											

Specific Lesson Skills											
Can make reasonable predictions.											
Can make detailed observations.											
Can propose an explanation.											
Can follow written directions.											
Can use a ruler and measure to the nearest centimeter and millimeter.											
Can work cooperatively with a partner or group.											
Can build on observations and data gathered by modifying investigations.											
Can design and create a graph based on data from investigations.											
Can use a magnifying glass.											
Can compare and contrast data.											
Can find mass to nearest gram.											
Can communicate through writing, drawing, and dialogue.											
Can apply what is learned to real-world situations.											

0-7682-3374-7 *Inquiry Science*

Name _____

Invertebrate Student Assessment

1. Complete the web to show what you have learned about earthworms.

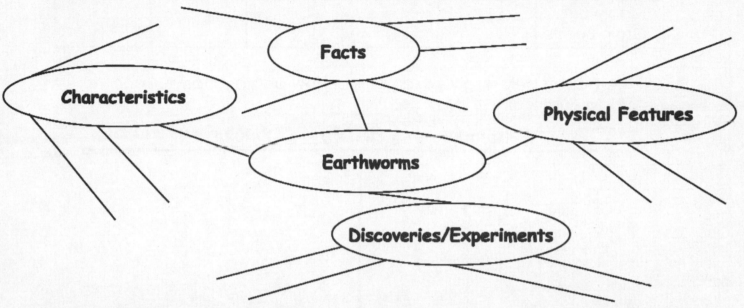

2. In the space below, label and draw each of the four stages of the mealworm. Write something you've learned about each stage below your drawings.

3. In the space below, write a short paragraph on how butterflies form.

_____

_____

_____

Published by Frank Schaffer Publications. Copyright protected.   0-7682-3374-7 *Inquiry Science*

4. On the chart below, compare a ladybug to a mealworm grain beetle.

	Size	Shape	Color	Movement	Other
Ladybug					
Mealworm Grain Beetle					

5. On the T-chart below, give examples of how ants are harmful and helpful to humans.

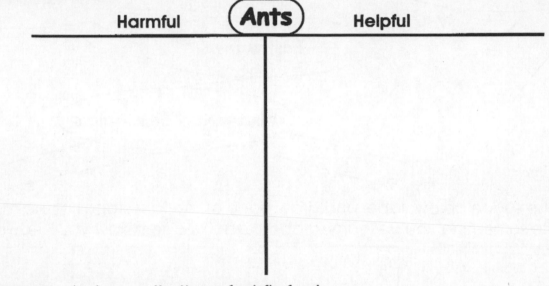

Harmful   (Ants)   Helpful

6. In the space below, write three fast-fly facts.

a. _____

b. _____

c. _____

7. In the space below, write three cool-cricket facts.

a. _____

b. _____

c. _____

8. Using the Venn diagram, compare and contrast snails to brine shrimp.

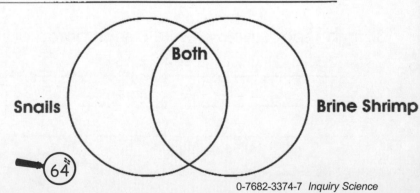

Both

Snails   Brine Shrimp

0-7682-3374-7 *Inquiry Science*

Weather

0-7682-3374-7 *Inquiry Science*

Weather Wisdom

Gearing Up

On a dry day, find an open pine cone in a tree. Hang the pine cone over a pan of simmering hot water and observe it over two hours. The moisture will cause the pine cone to close. Ask the students to hypothesize why the pine cone closed. Discuss that this is one sign from nature that the air is humid. People have used nature to predict weather in the past.

> ### Process Skills Used
> - analyzing
> - observing
> - communicating

Guided Discovery

Background for the teacher:

Weather is important because it affects every aspect of our lives. Throughout the ages, people have looked for patterns in nature and have devised creative stories to explain and forecast weather events. Today, weather forecasting is more scientific. Forecasters use computers, satellites, and precise instruments to predict the weather. But weather is a complicated science, and meteorologists still cannot be 100% accurate about the changing weather.

Directions for the activity:

Show a picture or drawing of a groundhog. Ask the students what this animal has to do with weather. Tell the story of the groundhog seeing its shadow on February 2. Discuss whether this is an accurate way to predict weather.

Have students fill out the activity sheet. Then discuss the answers.

Answer Key

1. True; a sudden change in air pressure may affect arthritic joints, bunions, even old wounds.
2. True; most animals feel changes in air pressure and feel uncomfortable and restless before a storm.
3. False
4. True; frogs are popular weather forecasters in almost every country.
5. True
6. True; skies are even a better predictor than animals. a red sky indicates a passing front.
7. False; but it may show the effects of a previous bad winter.
8. True; hot, humid nights mean rain.

Responding to Discovery

Divide the class into groups of eight. Provide each group with a large piece of bulletin board paper and crayons or colored markers. Instruct the students to draw eight puzzle pieces on the large paper. They will mark the top of each piece with a small X. Each student should cut out one piece and draw a picture of how weather affects their lives or makes them feel. When finished, the group can assemble their puzzle into a collage. Have each group discuss, then share and explain, their puzzle to the rest of the class.

Applications and Extensions

Investigate folk stories about weather from other cultures. Folklore is full of stories that relate to weather.

> ### Real-World Applications
> - Look up *biometeorology*, the branch of science that studies how weather affects living things.
> - Read about Theophrastus, the first Greek to study weather.

Name _____

Weather Wisdom

🐌 The following are sayings about weather. Write T, for *true*, if you think the saying has some basis in science. Write F, for *false*, if you think it has no basis in scientific fact. Be prepared to explain your choices.

_____ 1. An old timer says, "I can tell it's going to rain, my feet hurt."

_____ 2. When an old cat acts like a kitten, a storm is on the way.

_____ 3. Kill a snake and turn it on its belly for rain.

_____ 4. Frogs croak before a rain, but in the sun they stay quiet.

_____ 5. When bees stay close to the hive, rain is close by.

_____ 6. Red sky at night, sailor's delight—Red sky in morning, sailors take warning.

_____ 7. A tough apple means a hard winter is coming.

_____ 8. When the night has a fever, it cries in the morning.

🐌 Think about how weather affects you and complete the following.

Why do you think people want to predict the weather?

_____

_____

Give an example of when the weather might affect what you do.

_____

_____

When might the weather affect how you feel?

_____

_____

When do you talk about the weather?

_____

_____

Fill in the vowels e and o to spell the word for the science of weather.

M __ T __ __ R __ L __ G Y

Weather Begins with the Sun

Gearing Up

On a sunny day, take the class outside. Instruct the students to hold a magnifying glass over a piece of paper and bring the light to a point. (Caution students not to look directly at the point.) Have students observe what happens to the paper over several seconds. Discuss the results with the students. Discuss the power of the sun and the energy it creates in the form of heat and light.

> ### *Process Skills Used*
> - predicting
> - observing
> - forming a hypothesis
> - measuring
> - analyzing data
> - graphing

Guided Discovery

Background for the teacher:

Weather begins when the sun produces heat and light energy, called radiant energy. The following discovery demonstrates that the sun heats the earth unevenly and that different surfaces respond to the sun in various manners.

Materials for each group of four:

two (or four) jars   thermometers

aluminum foil   graph paper

black construction paper

Directions for the activity:

Experiment one: In each group, students fill two jars with equal amounts of water. They measure the starting temperature of the water, then place one jar in the sun and one in the shade. Ask students to predict how many degrees each jar of water will change after two hours.

Students measure the temperature of each jar of water at 20-minute intervals for two hours. Record the results, then create a bar graph displaying the data.

Experiment two: Have students fill two jars with equal amounts of water. Students will measure the temperature of each and cover one jar with aluminum foil (shiny side up) and the other with black paper. Students set the jars in direct sunlight and measure the temperature after 30 minutes to an hour.

Responding to Discovery

Students complete the activity sheets as they work. The two experiments may be done at the same time or consecutively. While students are waiting to measure temperature, discuss possible ways to graph their data. Discuss the results of both experiments as they relate to the manner in which the sun heats the earth.

Discuss the following questions:

- Why was the water in the sun a different temperature than the water in the shade?
- Why were the covered jars of water different temperatures?
- How is the black paper like soil? How is the aluminum foil like water?
- Does the sun heat the earth evenly? Explain.
- How might trees and forests affect the heating of the earth?
- What does uneven heating have to do with weather?

Applications and Extensions

Research with the class the benefits and applications of solar energy.

> ### *Real-World Applications*
> - Protection from the damaging rays of the sun.
> - Best clothes to wear in summer and winter.
> - Effects of global warming/greenhouse effect.

0-7682-3374-7 *Inquiry Science*

Weather Begins with the Sun

Does the sun heat the earth evenly?

1. Fill two jars with water and place one in the sun and the other in the shade. Measure and record the starting temperature. Predict the number of degrees the temperature will change in each jar after 2 hours. Then, measure the temperatures every 20 min. and record your data.

	Jar in the sun	Jar in the shade
Starting	°	°
Prediction	°	°
20 min.	°	°
40 min.	°	°
60 min.	°	°
80 min.	°	°
100 min.	°	°
2 hours	°	°

☙ On a sheet of graph paper, graph the data you collected.

☙ Write a hypothesis for why the temperatures changed. _____

_____

2. Fill two jars with water. Measure the starting temperature and cover one with aluminum foil (shiny side up). Cover the other jar with black paper. Set both jars in direct sunlight for 30 minutes to an hour.

   Starting temperature: Black paper _____ Foil _____

☙ Make a prediction: How do you think the water in the jar covered with aluminum foil will change in the sun? How will the jar covered with black paper change?

_____

☙ After 30 minutes to an hour, measure the temperature of the water in both jars.

   Black paper _____ Foil _____

Which color do you think absorbs heat best? _____

Which color reflects heat? _____

How does this relate to the heating of the earth? _____

_____

Write a hypothesis about how the uneven heating of the earth could affect weather.

_____

Sun as Air Mover

Gearing Up

Ask the students to think about a time when they walked barefoot across the sand on a hot day. What did they notice about the sand? It was probably very hot, and it made their feet hot. Tell students that heat energy from the earth has an effect on weather.

Process Skills Used
- observing
- forming a hypothesis

Guided Discovery

Background for the teacher:

The sun's energy is absorbed by the earth and transferred to the atmosphere in three ways: conduction, convection, and radiation. Convection involves the transfer of heat energy and the circulation of air currents. The air above the earth's surface gets heated, becomes less dense, and begins to rise. Cooler air moves in below. This cool air is heated by the ground and begins to rise. As the heated air rises higher into the atmosphere, it cools down and sinks. This cycle of moving warm and cool air (unequal heating) forms convection currents.

Materials for each team of four:

baby-food jar	food coloring
plastic wrap	rubber band
gallon (4L) jar or milk jug with the top cut off	
very hot water	ice water

Directions for the activity:

Students fill the small jar with very hot water (not hot enough to burn) and a few drops of food coloring. They should cover the jar tightly with plastic wrap and a rubber band and place it in the large jar. Then have students fill the large jar with very cold water. They should use a sharp pencil or other long pointed object to reach through the cold water and poke several holes in the plastic wrap. They may record their observations on the activity sheet.

Responding to Discovery

Discuss the movement of the water in the large jar. Ask students to relate that to the movement of hot and cold air in the atmosphere. Draw a diagram of the convection currents.

Have the students role play how molecules act when they are heated. The moving colored hot water will show students how heated molecules act.

Applications and Extensions

Have the students draw a picture of global wind systems or research the causes of "El Niño"

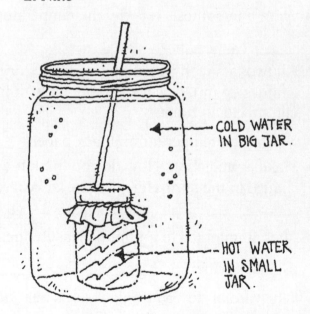

COLD WATER IN BIG JAR.

HOT WATER IN SMALL JAR.

Real-World Applications
- Ocean currents
- El Niño
- Trade winds

0-7682-3374-7 *Inquiry Science*

Name _____

Sun as Air Mover

(Why does air move?)

🌾 In your group, you will explore how hot and cold water act together. Think about how hot and cold air move as you observe the moving water.

Materials:
- baby-food jar
- food coloring
- plastic wrap
- gallon (4L) jar/milk jug
- 1 cup (240 mL) hot water
- 3 quarts (2.8 L) cold water

🌾 Directions for the activity:

1. Fill the small jar with very hot water and a few drops of food coloring. Tightly cover the small jar with plastic wrap and a rubber band.

2. Place the small jar inside the large jar. Fill the large jar with very cold water.

3. Use a sharp pencil or other long pointed object to poke a hole in the plastic wrap. Observe the colored water.

🌾 Draw three pictures of your experiment. Label each step.

🌾 Explain what happened to the colored water. _____

_____

🌾 Air in the atmosphere acts like a fluid. Explain how air moves over the heated earth.

_____

_____

_____

🌾 Why does air move? _____

_____

_____

0-7682-3374-7 *Inquiry Science*

Air Masses and Fronts

Gearing Up

Blow up two balloons. Ask the students to tell you attributes of the air inside the balloons. Lead the students to discover that the air has mass/weight. Tie a string to the center of a thin pole or light yard stick. Tape one balloon to each end of the pole. Have a student hold the string so the stick will balance. (You may need to adjust the position of the balloons to make them balance.) Put a piece of masking tape on one balloon and prick a hole through the tape into the balloon. (The tape will stop the balloon from popping.) Observe the pole as the air slowly leaks. Does it stay balanced? Have students explain what happened and relate it to how air acts in the atmosphere.

> ### *Process Skills Used*
> * observing
> * making a model
> * forming a hypothesis
> * inferring

Guided Discovery

Background for the teacher:

Air masses form when air remains over a region long enough to acquire the temperature and humidity of that region. Air masses move together but do not mix. The boundary between cold and warm air masses is called a front. When weather fronts meet, rain and violent weather form.

Materials needed for each student:

clear pint jar with lid

3/4-1 cup (180–240 mL) cooking oil

cold water

red and blue food coloring

Directions for the activity:

Have students fill the jar half full with cooking oil. Then add red food coloring and shake to mix. This represents a warm air mass. Have students add blue coloring to the cold water in a separate container. Have students predict what will happen when the two substances mix. Then gently pour the blue cold water into the jar of oil.

Have students place the screw cap tightly on the jar and slowly turn it on its side. Have them observe and describe how the liquid moves.

Responding to Discovery

Discuss the following questions to explore how the model relates to cold and warm fronts.

* Which liquid represents the warm front?
* Which represents the cold front?
* What happened when you poured cold water into oil?
* Which liquid is more dense?
* Which is more dense, warm or cold air?
* How did the behavior of this model compare with your prediction?

Applications and Extensions

Have students research types of fronts. They may work in groups to draw and label diagrams of the different fronts (warm front, cold front, warm-front occlusion, cold-front occlusion).

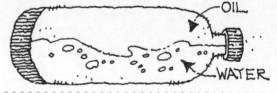

> ### *Real-World Applications*
> * How do parachutes behave in different air masses?
> * Discuss appropriate clothing for weather conditions.

0-7682-3374-7 *Inquiry Science*

Name _____

Air Masses and Fronts

What happens when warm and cold air masses come in contact?

☙ Warm air masses and cold air masses have different densities, just like oil and water. Observe how oil and water interact to simulate a front.

> **Materials:**
> - clear pint jar with lid
> - 3/4–1 cup (180–240mL) cooking oil
> - cold water in a separate container
> - red and blue food coloring

☙ Directions for the activity:

1. Fill the jar half-way with cooking oil. Add red food coloring and shake to mix. This represents a warm air mass.

2. Add blue food coloring to the cold water in a separate container. Predict what will happen when you mix the oil and water.

3. Gently pour the cold water into the jar of oil. Observe how the colored liquids react to each other. Cover tightly, turn the jar on its side, and observe how the liquids move. Move the jar gently in other ways.

☙ Draw two diagrams of your experiment. Label the drawings.

Describe how the liquids move. _____

_____

Which liquid is more dense? Explain. _____

_____

How does this model show what happens between air masses? _____

_____

Is warm or cold air more dense? _____

_____

0-7682-3374-7 *Inquiry Science*

Balloon Barometer

Gearing Up

Place two books (about 1-in/.25 cm thick) 3 in. (7.5 cm) apart on a table. Lay a sheet of paper across the books lengthwise. Ask students to predict what will happen when you blow under the paper into the space between the books. Record their predictions, then let the students try it. Repeat using a straw placed just under the edge of the paper. Discuss what happens.

3"

Process Skills Used

- observing
- predicting
- comparing
- recording data

Guided Discovery

Background for the teacher:

Daniel Bernoulli, a Swiss scientist in the 1700s, discovered that the faster a liquid or gas moves, the lower its pressure. The pressure below the paper in the gearing-up demonstration is lower than the pressure above, so the paper dips.

Air pressure changes with changes in temperature and elevation. Air pressure is measured by an instrument called a barometer. Students will make their own barometers and measure changes in pressure.

Materials needed for each group:

medium to large balloon
empty jar or can
heavy rubber band
sheet of unlined paper
broom straw (12 in./30 cm long)
strong glue such as silicone cement

Directions for the activity:

1. Inflate and deflate the balloon to stretch. Cut a piece of balloon large enough to cover the mouth of the can. Secure tightly with a rubber band.

2. Attach one end of the straw to the center of the balloon with glue so the straw is on its side.

3. Fold the paper so it can stand up on the table. Label with "High pressure" at the top of the paper (as shown).

4. Place the can near the folded paper with the pointer firmly up against it. Put a mark exactly where the straw touches the paper. Observe the barometer for five days, marking the location of the straw on the paper several times a day.

Responding to Discovery

Have students record their findings for five days. They should note the weather conditions outside and the level of the barometer and look for patterns. When the air pressure is higher outside the can than inside, the balloon will dip and the straw will move higher.

Applications and Extensions

Obtain a real barometer and explain how meteorologists use the instrument to measure air pressure and predict weather.

Have students explore other experiments related to air pressure. Invite a pilot to speak to the class about air pressure and weather.

Investigate Torricelli's mercury barometer.

Real-World Applications

- What does a flat bicycle tire have to do with air pressure?
- Discuss why a change in air pressure may affect the way some people act or feel.

0-7682-3374-7 *Inquiry Science*

Name _____

Balloon Barometer

> Can we measure air pressure?

❧ You observed a change in air pressure during the demonstration. How could you use that information to design your own barometer to measure air pressure? A balloon is flexible and will respond to changes in pressure.

Materials:

- medium to large balloon
- wide–mouth container such as a coffee can
- heavy rubber band
- sheet of unlined paper
- broom straw
- strong glue

❧ Directions for the activity:

1. Inflate and deflate the balloon to stretch it out. Cut out a piece of balloon large enough to cover the mouth of the can. Secure tightly with a rubber band.

2. Attach one end of the straw to the center of the balloon piece with glue so that the straw is lying on its side.

3. Fold the paper and stand it upright. Move the can next to the paper with the straw lightly against it. Put a red mark exactly where the straw touches. Record the location of the straw three times a day for five days. Label each mark with a symbol to indicate the time of reading.

❧ Keep a chart (below) of barometric pressure observations and the weather outside. Look for relationships. Mark changes in pressure with an arrow. (up, down, or side to side)

Barometer Reading			
	First Reading Time: _____	Second Reading Time: _____	Third Reading Time: _____	Weather Report
Day 1				
Day 2				
Day 3				
Day 4				
Day 5				

Were there any relationships between the readings and the weather? _____

_____

How accurate do you think your barometer is? _____

_____

Can you think of a way to improve the design? _____

0-7682-3374-7 *Inquiry Science*

Measuring Wind

Gearing Up

Make a copy of the poem "Who Has Seen the Wind" by Christina Georgina Rossetti.

> Who has seen the wind?
> Neither I nor you:
> But when the leaves hang trembling
> The wind is passing thro'.
> Who has seen the wind?
> Neither you nor I:
> But when the trees bow down their heads,
> The wind is passing by.

Read the poem and ask students about the wind. What is wind? Can you see the wind? How do you know it is there?

Process Skills Used

- recording data
- making a model
- measuring

Guided Discovery

Background for the teacher:

Meteorologists use an instrument called an anemometer to measure wind speed. The speed is measured in miles per hour, meters per second, or knots. In this activity, students will build their own devices to measure wind speed.

Materials needed for each group of four students:

four paper cups with handles—one should be a different color

a heavy plastic or paper plate

a stapler

a long push pin

a watch with second hand

a 1 cm diameter dowel or other thin stick

Directions for the activity:

Have students draw a straight line across the diameter of the plate and a second, perpendicular line. Students should draw a large dot where the lines intersect in the middle of the plate. They staple the handles of the four cups to the plate where the lines meet the edge of the plate, so that the openings of the cups face the same direction. Students insert the long pin through the center of the plate and the side of the dowel stick. The plate should move freely.

Have students secure the stick in the ground and watch the cups turn in the wind. They can measure wind speed by counting the number of revolutions the colored cup makes in a minute.

Responding to Discovery

Students will take three measurements of wind speed and find an average. Have student groups compare their data.

Show pictures of the ratings of wind on the Beaufort scale.

Discuss how the rating compares with the wind speed.

Applications and Extensions

Students research real anemometers. Find out what they look like, how they work, and where they are placed.

Real-World Applications

- Discuss Beaufort and his scale.
- Research famous weather vanes of the world.

Published by Frank Schaffer Publications. Copyright protected.

0-7682-3374-7 *Inquiry Science*

Name _____

Measuring Wind

How is wind speed measured?

❧ You cannot see the wind, but you can see its effects. Today you will make an anemometer to measure wind speed.

Materials:
- four paper cups with handles; one cup is a different color than the others
- a plastic or heavy paper plate
- a stapler
- a long pushpin
- a dowel or thin stick
- a watch with a second hand

❧ Directions for the procedure:

1. Draw two perpendicular lines across the front of the plate to find the center.
2. Staple the handles of the four cups to the edge of the plate where the lines meet the edge, so that the openings of the cups face in the same direction.
3. Insert the long pin through the center of the plate and then into the side of the dowel stick. Make sure your plate will move freely.

❧ Put your anemometer in the ground.
Count the number of rotations in 1 minute.
Repeat three times.

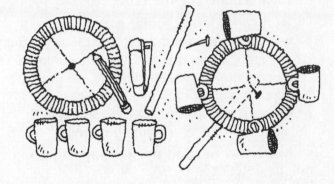

Trial 1 _____

Trial 2 _____

Trial 3 _____

Average revolutions per minute _____

Explain how you measure wind? _____

What is the name of the device used to measure wind? _____

❧ The Beaufort scale, designed by Admiral Francis Beaufort, puts numbers to different degrees of wind speed.

Beaufort Scale

calm day	0	(smoke goes straight up)
gentle breeze	3	(leaves and twigs move constantly)
strong breeze	6	(flags beat, umbrellas turn inside out)
strong gale	9	(slight damage to houses, awnings may rip)
hurricane	12	(excessive damage)

❧ Choose a number from 0–12 to describe the wind speed today. _____

0-7682-3374-7 *Inquiry Science*

Tornadoes and Hurricanes

Gearing Up

Pour a few spoonfuls of cornstarch and a drop of food coloring into a shallow pan of water. Ask the students to observe what patterns form. Very gently move a spoon through the water. Have students watch for a small vortex in the water. A vortex is a spiral of fluid pulling toward a center—like a small tornado. Add more coloring and observe what happens. Explain that air and water move in similar patterns.

> ### Process Skills Used
> • making a model
> • observing

Guided Discovery

Background for the teacher:

Hurricanes form circular patterns with winds flowing around a low pressure center or vortex. From the sky, a hurricane looks like a giant pinwheel spinning around. The "eye" is a calm area in the center of the raging storm. In this activity, students make a model of a swirling vortex.

Materials needed for a group of four:

two 2–liter pop bottles
tape
modeling clay
16" (40 cm) string
balloon
water
food coloring

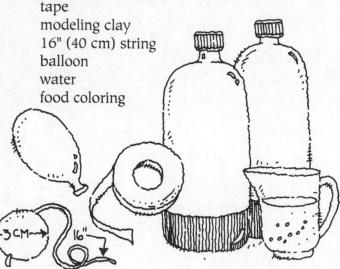

Directions for the activity:

Students follow the directions on page 79 to make a model simulating a hurricane. Students will try to suspend a piece of modeling clay in the center, or eye, of the hurricane. Before the activity, cut off the bottom of one of the pair of bottles and tape the edge. (The teacher should do this because of the use of sharp knives).

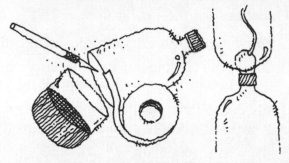

Responding to Discovery

Ask students to describe their hurricanes. Challenge them to get the hurricane swirling in both clockwise and counter clockwise direction. Ask students to hypothesize about why hurricanes swirl in opposite directions in the Northern and Southern Hemispheres.

Applications and Extensions

• Students make mini-presentations on violent weather conditions, such as thunder, lightning, snowstorms, hail, and cyclones.

• Students write and illustrate lightning safety rules.

> ### Real-World Applications
> • Research careers in meteorology.
> • Discuss storm films like "Twister."

0-7682-3374-7 *Inquiry Science*

Name _____

Tornadoes and Hurricanes

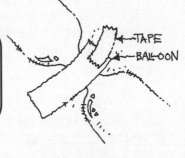

(How does a hurricane move?)

Materials:
- two 2-liter bottles (one with the bottom cut off)
- masking tape
- balloon
- modeling clay
- water
- 16" (40 cm) string
- food coloring

🖎 Directions for the activity:

(Your teacher has cut away the bottom end of one of the bottles and taped the edge.)

1. Make a 3-cm round ball of the modeling clay and fold in one end of the string. The string should be securely attached to the clay.

2. Join the bottles at the necks. Wrap a piece of balloon around the two necks and secure with tape. Use the ball of clay to plug the opening between the two bottles. It should be snug but not forced in. Hold onto the loose end of the string.

3. Turn the bottles so the cut end is up. Fill the top bottle over halfway with colored water. Move the device a circular motion. Then pull the plug and try to suspend the clay in the eye of the vortex.

🖎 Draw three diagrams of your experiment. Label the drawings.

What happened when you tried to suspend the clay in the eye of the vortex? Explain.

_____

_____

Empty the water and try the experiment again. What were your results?_____

_____

0-7682-3374-7 *Inquiry Science*

Water, Water Everywhere

Gearing Up

Today's discovery explores evaporation rates. Wipe a damp sponge across the chalkboard. Observe what happens for several seconds. Ask the students where the water went.

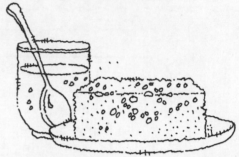

> ### Process Skills Used
> • predicting
> • comparing

Guided Discovery

Background for the teacher:

The sun's radiant energy turns liquid water into a gas, or water vapor. The liquid water comes from oceans, rivers, lakes, soil, plants, and animals. Wind moves the water vapor over the earth. Water vapor in the air is called humidity.

Materials needed for each group:

three waterproof plates

three colored markers

water

Directions for the activity:

Squeeze a dry sponge in front of the class to show there is no water in it. While one student holds the sponge up for the class to see, have another student pour one table-spoon of water at a time onto the sponge. Have students keep a tally of the number of spoonfuls of water the sponge absorbs before it drips. Ask if anyone knows what the word "saturated" means. Does anyone know what it is called when the sponge is full? Define the word "saturated" and explain that the air can also become saturated with water vapor. When the air is saturated, it has 100% humidity. Discuss where puddles go after a rain. Ask students to hypothesize about what causes water to turn into water vapor.

Students follow the directions on page 81 to compare evaporation rates in three areas: in direct sunlight, in the dark, and in the center of the classroom (not direct sunlight, but not dark). Discuss their predictions.

Responding to Discovery

Discuss the results as recorded on the activity sheets. Make models of solids, liquids, and gases using six Styrofoam balls and pipe cleaners. Fit the six balls snugly inside a circle of pipe cleaners to represent the molecular structure of a solid. Remove two balls to model the molecular structure of a liquid. Demonstrate to the students that the molecules can move much more freely in a liquid than in a solid. Take two more balls out to model the molecules in a gas. Point out that molecules can move around even more in a gas than in either a solid or a liquid.

Applications and Extensions

Discuss two hypothetical cities. The temperature is the same in both places. In one city, you immediately begin to perspire when you step outside. In the other you feel dry. Why?

> ### Real-World Applications
> • What happens to hair during humid weather?

0-7682-3374-7 *Inquiry Science*

Name _____

Water, Water Everywhere

> How does water get into the air?

- Gather your materials: three plates, three markers, and water

- Make a shallow puddle of water in each plate. Trace each puddle with the same color to indicate its size. Number the plates and place them in three different areas: direct sun, complete dark, and in the center of the classroom.

- Predict what will happen to the water in each plate:

Sun _____

Dark _____

Partly sunny _____

- Check the puddles after one hour. Trace each puddle with the second color marker. Describe how the puddles have changed.

_____

_____

- Check the puddles the next day. Trace each puddle with the third color marker. Draw pictures of your plates using the colors to show what happened.

Sun	Dark	Partly sunny

Which puddles shrank? _____

What do you think happened to the water? _____

_____

Why do you think the puddles shrank at different rates? _____

_____

What is the process called?   What is it called when the air is full of water?

E __ __ __ O __ __ T __ __ __   S __ __ __ __ __ __ __ D

In what three states does water exist?

_____   _____   _____

0-7682-3374-7 *Inquiry Science*

Milk Carton Hygrometer

Gearing Up

Set a few crystals of cobalt chloride* on a petri dish. After observing for a few minutes, ask the students what happened to the crystals. (The crystals absorbed water from the air and dissolved.)

Mix two tablespoons (30 mL) cobalt chloride and one tablespoon (15 mL) sodium chloride (table salt) with one cup (240 mL) of water. Stir to dissolve. Immerse strips of blotting paper in the solution. The strips will turn pink. Set the strips out to dry. As they dry, they will turn blue. After observing the change, ask the students what causes the change in color.

Hazard alert: *cobalt chloride is toxic by ingestion; practice strict hygiene in the use of this substance.*

*Cobalt chloride and other classroom chemicals can be obtained through Flinn Scientific, Inc. 800-452-1261

> ### *Process Skills Used*
> - observing
> - making a model
> - reading scientific tables

Guided Discovery

Background for the teacher:

Humidity is the term for water present in the air as water vapor. Relative humidity compares the water vapor in the air to the maximum amount of water vapor the air can hold at that temperature. Meteorologists measure relative humidity with a wet-bulb hygrometer. In this discovery, students will make a milk-carton hygrometer that measures relative humidity.

Materials for each group of four:

two room thermometers

quart (1 L) milk carton

thread

rubber bands

scissors

2" (5 cm) cotton strip

Directions for the activity:

Students follow the step-by-step directions for making a hygrometer. They collect data from the hygrometer and refer to a relative humidity table to find the current relative humidity.

Responding to Discovery

Students will complete page 83. Discuss the effects of humidity.

- Why do you think the temperature is different on the two thermometers?
- What does moisture in the air feel like?
- How do meteorologists use relative humidity in weather forecasting?
- What regions of the country have high humidity? Low humidity?

Applications and Extensions

Have students watch the weather report for a week. Have them maintain a chart of the relative humidity reading, the temperature, and the forecast.

> ### *Real-World Applications*
> - Discuss the role of perspiration in cooling the body. How does humidity affect the body's cooling process?

0-7682-3374-7 *Inquiry Science*

Name _____

Milk Carton Hygrometer

How can you tell how much water is in the air?

🌿 Directions for the activity:

1. Check the two thermometers to make sure they are at the same temperature.

2. Attach one end of a two-inch strip of cotton fabric with a string to the bulb of one thermometer. Let the cotton hang below the thermometer (as pictured).

3. Using two rubber bands, attach the thermometers to two sides of a milk carton (as pictured).

4. Cut a small hole in the carton just below the covered bulb and push the cotton tail through the hole. Fill the carton with water to just below the hole so the cotton tail is under water.

5. After several minutes, read the dry bulb and the wet bulb thermometers. Use the temperature of the dry-bulb thermometer (°F) and the difference between the two readings to find relative humidity (percentage) on the table.

🌿 Measure the relative humidity over several hours and then once a day for a week. Does the relative humidity change as weather conditions change?

Time/ Date of reading	Relative humidity
1	
2	
3	
4	
5	
6	
7	
8	
9	
10	
11	

Dry-Bulb Temperature °F

Wet-Bulb Temperature °F	56	58	60	62	64	66	68	70	71	72	73	74	75	76	77	78	79	80	82	84	86	88
38	7	2																				
40	15	11	7																			
42	25	19	14	9	7																	
44	34	29	22	17	13	8	4															
46	45	38	30	24	18	14	10	6	4	3	1											
48	55	47	40	33	26	21	16	12	10	9	7	5	4	3	1							
50	66	56	48	41	34	29	23	19	17	15	13	11	9	8	6	5	4	3				
52	77	67	57	50	43	36	31	25	23	21	19	17	15	13	12	10	9	7	5	3	1	
54	88	78	68	59	51	44	38	33	30	28	25	23	21	19	17	16	14	12	10	7	5	3
56		89	79	68	60	53	46	40	37	34	32	29	27	25	23	21	19	18	14	12	9	7
58			89	79	70	61	54	48	45	42	39	36	34	31	29	27	25	23	20	16	14	11
60				90	79	71	62	55	52	49	46	43	40	38	35	33	31	29	25	21	18	15
62					90	80	71	64	60	57	53	50	47	44	42	39	37	35	30	26	23	20
64						90	80	72	68	65	61	58	54	51	48	46	43	41	36	32	28	25
66							90	81	77	73	69	65	62	59	56	53	50	47	42	37	33	30
68								90	86	82	78	74	70	66	63	60	57	54	48	43	39	35
70									95	91	86	82	78	74	71	67	64	61	55	49	44	40
72											95	91	86	82	79	75	71	68	61	56	50	46
74													96	91	87	83	79	75	69	62	57	51
76															96	91	87	83	76	69	63	57
78																	96	91	84	76	70	64
80																			92	84	77	70
82																				92	84	77
84																					92	85
86																						92

What patterns did you observe? _____

_____

Why do you think one bulb must be wet to obtain this measurement? _____

_____

Challenge: How could you use cobalt chloride to measure humidity in the air?

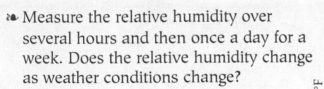

0-7682-3374-7 *Inquiry Science*

Condensation

Gearing Up

Fill a large, glass jar with boiling water and let it stand for two minutes. Pour out all but about 2 cups (480 mL) of the water. Hold a lighted splint in the jar for 2 seconds. Remove the splint and quickly put the lid on the jar. Place an ice cube on the lid. Ask the students to observe what happens and tell where they have seen something like this before.

Process Skills Used

- observing
- predicting
- making a model
- hypothesizing

Guided Discovery

Background for the teacher:

Condensation occurs as water vapor molecules cool, move closer together, slow down, and change to a liquid form. A cloud is made up of tiny drops of water condensed on the particles of dust or smoke.

Materials needed for each group of four:

glass cups or jars	ice cubes
water	paper clips
8–10 petri dishes	salt
4–5 canning jar lids	

Directions for the activity:

Students follow the directions on page 85 to observe the formation of condensation.

Responding to Discovery

Discuss what happened. (Drops condensed around the salt water.)

- What happened to the salt? Why? (Water evaporated causing high humidity around the salt, and the salt crystals dissolved in the water.)
- Review what happened with the puddle on the plate.
- Where does water go when it evaporates?
- What happened to the cold glasses? Ask students to explain their results and relate the findings to their understanding of condensation and the water cycle.

Applications and Extensions

Read the poem "Fog," by Carl Sandburg.

Have students write their own poems about fog, frost, or clouds.

Real-World Applications

- When and where do we see dew and frost?
- What are the hazards of foggy weather?

0-7682-3374-7 *Inquiry Science*

Name _____

Condensation

> How does condensation form?

In two different activities, your group will create conditions for condensation to form.

🔖 Directions for Experiment 1:

Materials: a clear glass jar, water, and ice

1. Observe a glass jar that has been resting at room temperature.
   Write your observations about how it feels (wet, dry, warm, cool).

   _____

2. Fill the jar with ice and water. How does the jar feel on the outside?

   _____

   _____

3. Leave the jar full of ice water for about half an hour. Then, write your observations
   about how the outside of the jar feels._____

   _____

4. Explain how water appeared on the outside of the jar. _____

   _____

5. Leave the jar overnight. Then, write your observations about how the outside
   of the jar feels the next day. _____

   _____

🔖 Directions for Experiment 2:

Materials: a covered petri dish, two paper clips, and a canning jar lid

1. Place the paper clips inside the petri dish. Pour a thin layer of water into the dish.
   Rest the canning jar lid on top of the paper clips. Shake about 6–10 salt crystals
   onto the lid.
2. Do not let the lid get wet.

What do you think will happen when you cover the petri dish and observe for about a
half hour? _____

What do you notice around the salt? _____

Where did it come from? _____

Where have you seen something like this before? _____

0-7682-3374-7 *Inquiry Science*

Rain Maker

Gearing Up

Put a transparency on an overhead projector. Ask one student to use a dropper full of water to make several drops in a straight line on the transparency. Ask another student to use the point of a pencil to drag the drops together. Repeat several times with different students. Discuss what happens.

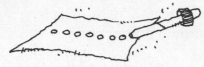

Process Skills Used

- observing
- predicting
- inferring
- making a model

Guided Discovery

Background for the teacher:

Water molecules are attracted to each other. As water vapor molecules accumulate together in the clouds, the clouds are overcome by gravity and precipitation falls from the sky. This precipitation may take the form of rain, snow, sleet, hail, or drizzle. Review the concepts of evaporation, condensation, and precipitation as parts of the water cycle.

Materials for each group of four:

one quart (liter) jar with lid

boiling water

ice cubes

Directions for the activity:

Ask students to predict what will happen in the following discovery. Place a jar in the center of each group/table. Add enough boiling water to cover the bottom of the jar. Carefully place the lid upside down on the mouth of the jar. Place three ice cubes on the inverted lid. Have each group observe the jar for 5 minutes.

Responding to Discovery

Students write their observations on the activity sheet every minute for five minutes.

Discuss how their observations compare to their predictions.

Applications and Extensions

Read the poem "Little Raindrops" by Jane Euphemia Browne. Discuss changes in feelings during changes in weather.

Use a rain gauge to measure precipitation.

Real-World Applications

- Discuss acid rain and its effects.
- Explain the process of seeding clouds to make rain.
- Discuss the role of rain in agriculture.

0-7682-3374-7 *Inquiry Science*

Name _____

Rain Maker

❧ Prediction: What do you think will happen when ice cubes are put on top of the jar of hot water? _____

_____

❧ Draw two pictures of the jar of hot water—one as soon as the ice is placed on top and one after 5 minutes. Write your observations below.

❧ Observations:

1 minute _____

2 minutes _____

3 minutes _____

4 minutes _____

5 minutes _____

❧ Why do you think the hot water and ice reacted the way they did? _____

_____

❧ List some elements of the water cycle.

_____

_____

❧ Explain the process of the water cycle.

_____

_____

_____

_____

0-7682-3374-7 *Inquiry Science*

Water in a Circle

Gearing Up

On a sunny day that follows a rainy or wet day, give each group of students a clear jar to put upside down in a grassy, sunny area. Ask the students what they think will be in the jar when they come back in a couple hours. When you return, there should be condensation in the jar. Discuss where the water came from and review the concepts from the previous lessons: evaporation, precipitation, and condensation.

Process Skills Used
- observing
- making a model

Guided Discovery

Background for the teacher:

Water vapor condenses and falls to the ground as precipitation. Water returns to the air by evaporation from the land, rivers, and oceans, or by plant transpiration. All water on earth enters the atmosphere as water vapor at some time. The earth's water is continually cycled through the water cycle. No new water is ever produced.

Materials needed for each group:

a clear, plastic container with lid
 (like the kind you would get from a deli)

soil and water

fast germinating seeds such as marigold, herbs, or lima beans

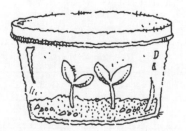

Directions for the activity:

Students plant seeds in the closed container. They observe the water cycle in action and record their observations with labeled diagrams.

Responding to Discovery

After five days, have students take the lids off of the containers and feel the soil. Discuss why the soil is still wet.

Make the connection between the real world and their terrariums.

- What in the real world is like the seeds?
- What in the real world is like the water collecting on the lids?

Discuss where water in the clouds comes from.

Applications and Extensions

Have students write a one-page story on the travels of Wanda or Willie the Water Molecule as he or she travels through the rain cycle. Encourage students to be creative. For example, the drop could be in the snow that fell on George Washington at Valley Forge.

Real-World Application
- What is the role of wetlands?
- Discuss the crisis of the rain forests.

0-7682-3374-7 *Inquiry Science*

Name _____

Water in a Circle

How does the water cycle work?

🖝 Directions for the activity:

1. Gather materials: container with lid, 2 cups (480 mL) soil, 3–6 seeds, and water

2. Put an inch (2.5 cm) of soil in the bottom of the container. Plant the seeds according to package. Soak with water.

3. Put the lid on the container and place it in a sunny window.

4. Watch your terrarium for several days. Write your observations. Draw and label a picture of your terrarium each day.

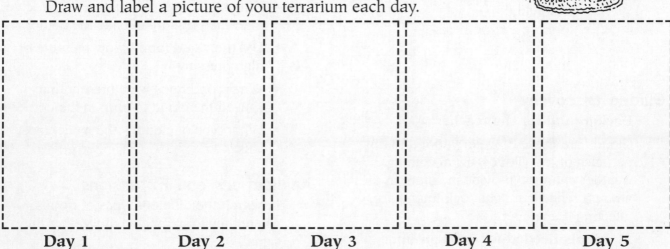

| Day 1 | Day 2 | Day 3 | Day 4 | Day 5 |

Observations: _____

_____

_____

_____

🖝 Draw a diagram of the water cycle and label the parts. Include the terms *evaporation*, *condensation*, and *precipitation*.

0-7682-3374-7 *Inquiry Science*

Clouds

Gearing Up

On a foggy day, ask the students if they would like to touch a cloud. Take students outside and compare fog to a cloud. Explain that fog is a cloud that forms close to the ground. On a sunny day, take students outside to observe cloud shapes. Ask students what they think the clouds can tell about the weather.

Guided Discovery

Background for the teacher:

Clouds are made of water vapor and tiny particles of ice. Clouds signal coming weather changes, provide moisture in the air, and reflect sunlight back into space, affecting the temperature.

Materials needed for each group:

2–liter soft-drink bottle with screw-on cap

cup of hot water (not hot enough to burn)

funnel

lit candle (handled by the teacher) to create smoke

Directions for the activity:

Instruct students to pour hot water into the bottle through the funnel, then cover and shake the bottle. Have students squeeze and release the bottle. Discuss where low pressure and high pressure occurred inside the bottle.

Have students uncap and squeeze the bottle. Blow out the candle and hold the smoking end over the mouth of the bottle while the students stop squeezing and quickly cap the bottle. (This draws the smoke inside.)

Instruct students to observe the bottle.

Have the students try squeezing the bottle to change the amount of pressure inside.

Responding to Discovery

Discuss the following questions:

- When is the pressure in the bottle lower than the pressure outside the bottle?
- Did the cloud form in low pressure or high pressure?
- What conditions were present that caused the cloud to form in the bottle?
- What type of cloud is the model most like?

Applications and Extensions

Research the different types of clouds, where they form, and what weather they signal.

Name _____

Clouds

> What are clouds?

Today you will explore the conditions that cause clouds to form. Think about how you could vary the experiment to determine exactly what causes the clouds to form. Think of varying water temperature, container shape or size, pressure, and quantity of smoke or water.

Directions:

1. Use the funnel to pour the cup of hot water into the bottle. Cover and shake the bottle.

2. Squeeze the covered bottle and release. When does the bottle have low pressure and when does it have high pressure?

   _____

   _____

3. The teacher will come to your group with smoke for the experiment.

4. Uncap and squeeze the bottle. The teacher will hold the smoking candle over the mouth of the bottle. Stop squeezing and quickly cap the bottle. (This draws the smoke inside.)

5. Record your observations and draw a diagram.

   _____

   _____

   _____

   _____

   _____

6. Try some variations of the experiment and record your observations.

   _____

   _____

   _____

7. What conditions caused the cloud to form?

   _____

Weather Prediction

Gearing Up

View a segment of a weather report from television (live or taped). Ask the students to take notes and be prepared to ask and answer questions about what they see. What percentage of the news time was spent on predictions, compared to reports of known weather conditions? To what instruments does the meteorologist refer? Is there any severe weather forecasted? Were clouds mentioned? What precipitation or humidity was reported or predicted?

> **Process Skills Used**
> - observing
> - interpreting data
> - comparing

Guided Discovery

Background for the teacher:

Many meteorologists work as weather observers. They measure weather conditions using a variety of scientific instruments. The observations are taken on land, in the air, and at sea. Satellites take pictures of the earth from above. All this information is used as evidence to describe and predict the behavior of the weather.

Other meteorologists forecast weather and warn people about coming changes in weather and hazardous conditions.

Directions for the activity:

Have students bring in weather maps from the newspaper. Have students work in pairs to compare maps. They should look for similarities and differences. Are there some symbols that all weather maps use? Are there some symbols that are unique? Have students cut out the key to the symbols. Then, have them complete the activity sheet on page 94.

Responding to Discovery

Have each pair of students report their findings about the weather maps. Ask students to tell what impact the weather has on their daily lives.

Applications and Extensions

Have students set up a class weather station using the instruments they have created or purchased instruments. Have students keep a log of weather conditions and give periodic weather reports.

> **Real-World Application**
> - Visit a local weather station.
> - Research careers in meteorology.

0-7682-3374-7 *Inquiry Science*

Weather Prediction

(What makes up a weather report?)

❧ Study two different weather maps. List the features that are the same.

_____

_____

❧ List the features that are different.

_____

_____

❧ Study your maps to answer the following questions.

1. Where can you find a measure of air pressure? _____

_____

2. What is the symbol for wind direction? _____

3. What is the symbol for wind speed? _____

4. What does H mean? _____

5. What does L mean? _____

6. What do the different colors on the map mean? _____

_____

❧ Tape the key from your weather map here.

❧ After studying your weather map, write a weather report as it might be told on the television or radio.

_____

_____

_____

_____

_____

_____

Performance-Based Assessment

3 = Exceeds expectations
2 = Consistently meets expectations
1 = Below expectations

Lesson Investigation Discovery	Student Names									
Lesson 1: Weather Wisdom										
Lesson 2: Weather Begins with the Sun										
Lesson 3: Sun as Air Mover										
Lesson 4: Air Masses and Fronts										
Lesson 5: Balloon Barometer										
Lesson 6: Measuring Wind										
Lesson 7: Tornadoes and Hurricanes										
Lesson 8: Water, Water Everywhere										
Lesson 9: Milk Carton Hygrometer										
Lesson 10: Condensation										
Lesson 11: Rain Maker										
Lesson 12: Water in a Circle										
Lesson 13: Clouds										
Lesson 14: Weather Prediction										

Specific Lesson Skills										
Can make reasonable predictions.										
Can make detailed observations.										
Can propose an explanation.										
Can write a hypothesis.										
Displays curiosity.										
Can work cooperatively with a partner or group.										
Can read measurement and weather instruments.										
Can create a graph with data from investigations.										
Can follow written directions.										
Can communicate through writing and drawing.										
Can apply what is learned to real-world situations.										

0-7682-3374-7 *Inquiry Science*

0-7682-3374-7 *Inquiry Science*

0-7682-3374-7 *Inquiry Science*